I dedicate this book to some of the best friends
a person could have in this world.

Howard Strasler and Marvin Grover were two of mine.

Phil. 1:6

Keep on Laughing
John A. Walker

b

Printed by:
A&J Printing
P.O. Box 518
Nixa, MO 65714

Published by: J.A.W.'S Publishing

Order From:
Sgt. John A. Walker
530 Alger Ave.
Manistique, MI 49854
Phone: 906-341-2082
E-mail: jawspub@juno.com

Library of Congress Cataloging-In-Publication Data
Walker, John A.

ISBN 0-9639798-7-6

1th printing

Sgt. John A. Walker writes for:
Manistique Pioneer Tribune
212 Walnut St.
Manistique, MI 49854
Phone: 906-341-5200

These stories are written to show the humorous side of working as a Game Warden- living in Michigan U.P. They are not meant to offend anyone and are just the writer's version of the stories as he heard or saw them happen. No names are used in the stories without prior approval.

The U.P.
Upper Michigan

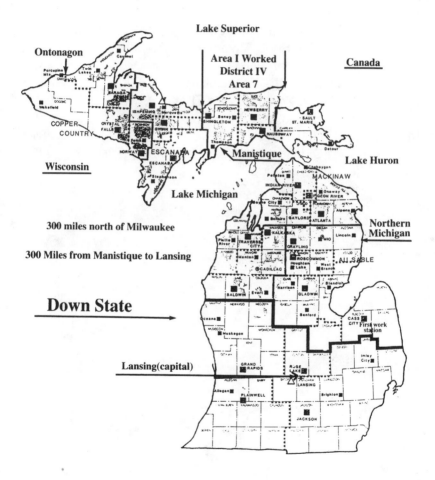

d

INDEX

Conservation Officer's Stories
Upper Michigan Tales from a Game Warden's Perspective

"Whatdaya Mean A Bad Attitude?"

Forewarned

Sgt. Walker still sits in amazement after, going through more than 70,000 copies of his first six books, at how well they have sold to people from all walks of life.

When you write a weekly article for a small town newspaper (Manistique Pioneer Tribune) in the middle of Michigan's U.P. who would have ever thought his success would be what it has been?

Who would have ever thought that a Michigan Conservation Officer starting out listening to the old time officers tell stories of their adventures would become the author of six books?

Sitting beside his grandfather listening to the way stories were told back in the 40's and 50's was maybe the best education Sgt. Walker could have ever received in the art of story telling. Before the TV arrived when families got together they would spend hours sitting there reliving the great memories of the past.

Later while working as a Michigan Conservation Officer Sgt. Walker once again spent hours and hours listening to some of the greatest storytellers on the great outdoors there were.

Whenever a crew of Game Wardens got together there would be stories told until the wee hours of the morning. A lot of the things talked about would only happen once in a lifetime, because there is no way a person could screw up that bad twice in one lifetime.

Of course with a good storyteller the stories only got better and better as the years went along. This is what makes a great story worth retelling.

f

The style of story telling, in the previous six books that Sgt. Walker has published, must be liked by someone because he has sold more than 70,000 copies of these *Tales From A Game Warden* books.

A number of Sgt. Walker's books have qualified to be placed on a self-publisher's best sellers list. His first book alone titled *A Deer Gets Revenge* has sold more than 25,000 copies.

There is a feeling that one of the reasons Sgt. Walker's books have sold so well is the fact that the stories are told just like his grandfather would sit and tell tales to his grandkids. Needless to say his grandfather never thought of using any bad language while telling these stories to his grandchildren.

In this day and age when there have been so many changes maybe there was just the right nitch for someone like Sgt. Walker to come forward with his style of humorous, family-style, outdoor tales.

The scholarship fund which was started with the help of the sales from the books in the *Tales From A Game Warden* series has been able to give out more than $20,000 to college students attending Christian Colleges. The scholarship fund itself has more than $20,000 in the account to help more young people that need it.

Sgt. Walker keeps saying each time he comes out with a new book, "This is the last one." But he keeps going on account of the hundreds of requests he gets for any new book before it even comes out. He now says number 7 is the last one because number 7 is supposed to be a perfect number.

But, we will have to just wait and see.

The Cover

The bear pictured on the cover of this book is the pet black bear of Dean Oswald up at Oswald's Bear Ranch north of Newberry, Michigan.

Tyson weighed 880 pounds when he died in the spring after having a fight for dominance with a much younger bear. He was 12 years old at the time. Dean figured that Tyson weighed more than 1,000 pounds when he went into hibernation in the fall.

The bear he fought was Cody that weighed more than 600 pounds at the time.

The Oswald's bear ranch is one of the most amazing places I have ever had the opportunity to go to. I have watched the faces of people from a grandmother to a young child just stand in amazement as they watched some of the young bear horse play around.

What better toy could an x-marine have for a pet than a 1,000-pound black bear?

You can read the story on Dean Oswald in chapter 8.

h
Dear Friend,

I guess there is no way that I deserve all the blessings I have received in my life. God has been so good to me. I listened to my Dad while growing up and ended up with the job I always wanted since my high school days. While in the army I met and married my wife and God blessed us with four wonderful children. Now we have seven grandchildren. I could go on and on talking about the blessings of God, but there is something more important I would like to tell you about. While in the army a friend gave me a book titled "The Greatest Story Ever Told". I read this book and it really got me thinking. Later I read the book called "What would Jesus do?" From these two books I started to wonder about Jesus dying on the cross once for all and I realized that all included me. After meeting my wife I asked the Lord to forgive my sins and come into my heart, but there was always a little question in my heart about being saved. A couple of years later I attended some special meetings being preached by a bear hunting friend of mine Evangelist Pete Rice. During these meetings I made sure about my salvation and have never had this doubt in my heart again.

Once I heard Brother Pete preach on John 3:16 "For God so loved the world that he gave his only begotten son, that whosoever believeth in Him should not perish, but have everlasting life". At the end of his preaching six people walked the isle to get saved. One was a tough, old, trapper that I knew and it really impressed me. What does being saved mean? It simply means that one understands that Jesus came and died on the cross for our sins, that we understand we are a sinner, and we ask Jesus to come into our heart, forgive our sins, and be our Savior.

You can use what is called the Romans Road to help you with this. It is as easy as driving down a 2-track out in the woods. If you would take a Bible you would find these verses. Romans 3:23 "All have sinned and come short of the glory of God." This means that all people have sinned and need to realize it. Romans 6:23 states, "the wages of sin is death". This means if we do not ask forgiveness of God for our sins we will die with payment due for them. I Corinthians 15:3 says, "Christ died for our sins". This means payment has already been paid in full for our sins by Jesus death on the cross. Romans 6:23 tells us, "the gift of God is eternal life through Jesus Christ our Lord". Everything that has to be done has been done, but for our part. Romans 10:13 tells us how, "Whosoever shall call upon the name of the Lord shall be saved". This means all a person has to do is understand they are a sinner, that Jesus died on the cross for them, and ask Him to come into their heart and forgive their sins. Then you like so many before you will have ever lasting life to look forward to.

I pray you will do this and someday I will see you in heaven and you can tell me about it.

Chapter 1
Conservation Officer's Stories **Upper Michigan Tales from a Game Warden's** **Perspective**
Honest There Is A Season

It is totally amazing how many things in life are true, only 99% of the people out there figure that there is no way that could really be the case. In my travels as a game warden there were always those that liked a good laugh. In fact there were those that would go out of their way to find one. The story below is one such case when the prosecutor's secretary found out there really was such a season and wanted her boss to realize it.

Life can be a lot of fun if you let it be. The other day I was reading some stuff that I have not looked at for years. In one section of the law I came across a section that re-confirmed my opinion of the ACLU and most people's opinion of lawyers. Back in the olden days the Conservation Department had the right idea. When the laws were passed they placed a season on lawyers.

In Act 165 of 1929, *The people of the State of Michigan enact:* Sec. 1-a Open seasons by species: *in it shall be unlawful for any person to take, catch or kill, or attempt to take, catch or kill any species named this section which this state has jurisdiction except during the following open seasons:*

Under section (f) it then reads: *lawyers and sheepshead may be taken at all seasons of the year in waters that are open.*

After reading this I got to thinking, you know maybe there is a reason that you never see lawyers out at a public beach swimming. Because if you read this section real close, the only time you can really take a lawyer, even if the season is open all year-round, is when they are in the water. It totally amazed me how much wisdom our forefathers must have had.

Seriously, if you sit down and read some of the old laws as I have been doing you would be amazed at all the things that are in them. In fact there are a number of laws on the books that if we had used them like they were supposed to be applied back at the turn-of-the-century, we would not have some of the problems we have today with the environment. Now we have umpteen more laws trying to do what these laws could have prevented if they had been applied. I don't think you can ever pass enough laws to give someone a brain and the ability to use one, if all they have in the first-place is an empty cranium.

A good example of a law that has been on the books for years and never enforced that we are now paying for is found in Act 350, Laws of **1865** that reads as follows: 6422 *Unlawful dumping into waters; Sec.10 It shall be unlawful for any person or persons to put into said waters any sand, coal, cinders, ashes, log slabs, decayed wood, bark, sawdust, or filth.* Why we have so many rivers filled with waste from sawmills is beyond me when this law was on the books since 1865.

Really now from what I am told a lawyer is really a member of the burbot family and are really, really, **really** ugly! This makes them a member of the freshwater codfish family. Now if you grew up when I did you learned to question anything that came close to cod liver oil that came in a green, slimy, colored liquid in a brown bottle. You had to hold your nose and take a spoon of this each morning.

Could this be the reason that most people and commercial fishermen that caught a lawyer just left it laying out on the ice for the birds?

At Least There Used to Be!

It sure is funny when you stop and think of all the laws that we already have and each year more and more comes down the shute. There is no way we are ever going to pass enough laws to make everybody happy and cover every situation. The last couple of months I have reread some old laws that were on the books for years that nobody realized were there.

In the early part of the last century (Did you ever think you would be around to be able to write a statement like this?) there was a law on the books that read: The Conservation Commission is hereby authorized to fix an open season for the taking of beaver and otter under such rules and regulations as shall by it be deemed expedient.

The following animals are not protected by this act and may be taken at any time, in accordance with the provisions of this act: Listed under this section of this act were house cats! I always figured this was a great law and it made a whole lot of sense to me. But as usual there were those that found that house cats should have "rights" too and the law was changed.

I can remember reading a report years ago where someone had kept track of a house cat that was one of those that the owners would let out at night and find the sweet little thing sleeping on the back steps each morning waiting to be let back in.

This party did a study on what this house cat brought home each morning after his night of hunting. You would be amazed how many baby game birds, rabbits, songs birds and such this house cat managed to catch while out "sleeping" on their porch each night. It is one of those studies that I read in an old publication that I wish I could remember where I saw it.

But needless to say a cat of any kind is really a hunter, so when left where they can fulfill their natural instincts they will always do it. They are no different than anything else on this earth.

Maybe There Should Be!

As if the people that live up here in Yooperland did not have enough things to think about, now the official word is out that we have something new to look forward to! For years normal, (debatable) everyday Yoopers have been reporting spotting these creatures in their travels and nobody paid much attention to it. In fact I had reports of two locals seeing one up off Thunder Lake Road a few years ago. But naw, these were just Yoopers after a hard day seeing things.

In fact while attending an outdoor show over in Escanaba, this man and his wife came up to talk to me. Right away I realized they had a lot of class and showed extreme wisdom because they purchased a set of my books. As we talked I found out these people lived in New York now and had traveled all over the world. As we were talking the lady said, "Let me ask you something, are there cougars in this area?" Then she told me this story.

They own property down on the Stonington Peninsula and have a large motor home they park down there when they are up here in the U.P. She said she had let their dogs out, two Poodles (naturally if you live in New York), this morning and was standing in the window of their motor home watching them, when she saw something out of the corner of her eye. All of a sudden she realized there was a cougar, or mountain lion, or whatever, coming into the opening where her two New York Poodles were!

She ran to the door to call the dogs in while her husband grabbed for the camera to try to get a picture of this large cat. Needless to say it just kept on going through the opening and they never got a picture of it. Being me, I told her what she ought to do was stake her two New York Poodles out in the yard for bait and sit there with her camera until this cougar returned. Then she could get a good picture of the cougar. She would then be famous and settle a long debated question. She gave me that, "You can't be serious look." I figured maybe I should have suggested using her husband for bait instead of her two New York Poodles and she may have went for it.

Now in the last week I have received two different articles flat telling us there are cougars running around in Michigan. Especially here in the U.P. There have always been reports of cougar sightings as long as I worked as a game warden. But now seeing one was spotted in Schoolcraft County by a college professor articles are written about these large cats. Farmers have spotted them, Red Owl Store owners have spotted them, pulp cutters have spotted them, but not until an "Exspurt", a college professor from **down** state sees one do we finally see articles that there are cougars living in Michigan. Does this not tell you something?

I can see why nobody believed the retired forester that this article talks about; this was one of the best jokes, laughed about for years within the DNR. The cougar Exspurt! But for years he collects and checks on all the reports from people who claimed to have observed cougars here in the U.P. I hate to admit it, but if now it is officially decided that there are really cougars living here amongst us here in Yooperland we just may have to give our now retired forester cougar Expsurt some credibility.

In fact a large number of the sightings were right here in

Schoolcraft and Delta Counties. So now if you see something that you were really not quite sure you saw or (should admit seeing at coffee,) because nobody would ever believe you even if you were sure you saw it, you can now say you did see it! Nobody will ever believe you anyway, but that has nothing to do with trying to tell people you saw a Mountain Lion out in the woods the other day. In other words as the articles states, "Cougars are back, in fact they never left!"

But as an old Game Warden I do have to wonder why with all the dog hunters up here in the U.P. there has never been a case, that I heard of, where a crew running their dogs after Bobcat ever treed a Cougar? Does it not seem that with all the hours these men spend out there running their dogs they would at one point or another come across a Cougar in their travels? At least once?

First, here is a picture of a nut. An English walnut.

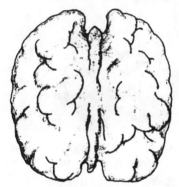

Second, here is a picture of a human brain.

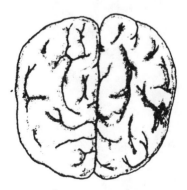

A comparison of the two helps make human behavior a little easier to understand.

This is Tyson a black bear that weighed more than 800 pounds when he died in the spring, but was well over 1,000 when he went into hibernation. This was one of the pet bear of Dean Oswald.

Chapter 2
Conservation Officer's Stories
Upper Michigan Tales from a Game Warden's Perspective
Strange, But True

Some things in life you could never make happen, in fact they will never happen again because they were so strange that all the pieces would never fit into place to let them. Below are a few tales of things that happened to hunters that were told to this old game warden. The only problem was, in the case of the first story, they told me how it worked **after** I was retired!

Run That By Me Again!

In order to sell a few of my books I attend some outdoor shows around the state. I ran into a party down at the outdoor show in Traverse City one weekend that gave me some good scientific advice, only too late seeing I'm now retired.

This party told me he grew up in the last house on Cedar Street, in the town where I worked as a game warden, years ago before he moved downstate to find work. He gave me this piece of information that I have yet to study the scientific value of personally. But when I walk into Jacks at coffee time I may just whistle, just try it out and see what happens.

He told me, "If you whistle, like you do out in the woods to get a deer to hesitate for a second so you can get a good shot at it, and someone who lives on Tannery Road ears twitch like a deer's ears do, it means they have been eating venison quite regularly." "Their genes are so full of venison in this neighborhood that you think maybe it's become hereditary for their ears to twitch!" In fact he told me that they have been eating venison for so long that this is just a natural reaction and they cannot stop their ears from twitching when you whistle.

Now I didn't come up with this! Someone who grew up here in the U.P. and said they used to do it all the time at school and it really works told it to me! What can I say? It came from a former Yooper Native who grew up on Cedar Street and if you can't believe some-

8

one off Cedar Street, whom can you believe in this day and age?

Shoot It! Shoot It! Before It Kills Me!

One weekend I went to Paradise to the *Wild Blueberry Festival*. In all my travels around peddling my books I never ran into something like this before. Now you have to understand that Cooks and Gulliver have more streets than Paradise does. When you get to Paradise you have to travel one of two ways. You are either coming into town or leaving town because after you hit that mid-point of their only street you go from doing one to the other.

The people of Paradise put on this *Wild Blueberry Festival* each year and they have an art and craft sale as part of it. You would not believe the people from all over the country that end up there for this weekend. In fact I soon found out that for some reason blueberries and my *"Tales From a Game Warden"* books must go together. In fact I would have those few skeptics about the quality of the stories of my books know that I sold a complete set to a college professor! In fact he is the director of the Honors Program at the University of Alabama! In fact his wife works at the space center down there. Are they going to be impressed or what? Well maybe you better not answer that.

In my travels I came across this story while up there.

This should maybe fall under "Kill it Quick".

It seems that there was this hunter that knew where there was this nice buck with a big rack that he would sure like to get. This hunter was big enough to, as the saying goes, kill a bear with a switch. He went at least 6'7" and weighted a conservative 285.

During the hunting season he decided to take a buddy and go out and see if his luck would allow him a chance at this super buck. As luck would have it sure enough he saw this buck and got a good shot at it. But needless to say as most big bucks do, it did not drop right there, so he had to wait awhile, get his buddy, and then they went out looking for it.

While tracking this monster they came to a point where they had to split up to try and figure out which way his dream buck went after being shot. As he poked through the woods, all of a sudden he saw his dream rack lying on the ground right in front of him! He slowly walked up to his deer and just stood there admiring the large rack on this buck.

He set his gun against a tree, straddled the buck, and then reached down, as they do on all the TV shows, and seized the rack on both sides to hold it up so he could get a better look and just admire it for a minute. It was everything he knew it would be. Some dreams do come true.

All of a sudden he was no longer admiring his trophy buck, but was now riding it!

It seems that when he reached down to grab the rack, just when he stepped across the back of the dead deer, which was not really dead at all. The buck suddenly came back to life!

So now our 6'7", 285-pound hunter, turned rodeo rider, was now taking off on the ride of his life. He managed to get stabbed in the side by an antler and also one long gash in his arm, as he screamed for his buddy, who was coming through the woods towards him, to come and help him out!

With all the points on this large buck flying back and forth, left and right, there was no way he dare let go! Finally his buddy came running through the woods as he kept yelling at him, "Finish killing this thing! Finish Killing this thing! Before it kills me!"

Hold It, I Haven't Taken a Picture Yet!

On the lighter side in my travels of course, I manage to come across a few new hunting tales. It seems there was this deer hunter out after the big one when as luck would have it he managed to drop a real nice buck. He walked over to where this trophy buck lay on the ground and stood there for a few minutes in unbelief as to how big and wide the rack on this buck was!

Finally he realized he had to get ready to do the work part of getting a deer, so he looked for a place to put his rifle and hang up his coat while he cleaned the buck. As he reached into his hunting coat he remembered he had one of those throwaway cameras in his pocket. After thinking a minute (You must understand that this had to be one of those Trolls that live down under the bridge.) he figured he might as well get some good pictures with his monster buck in the normal setting where he had dropped it before he started to clean his deer.

So our hunter took his hunting rifle and set it across the nice rack on the buck and wrapped the sling on the rifle around the antlers on the buck. Then he hung his hunting coat off one of the points on the antlers so he could get a couple of nice pictures. Pictures like the ones you always see those successful hunters showing at those outdoor shows on TV.

He later said that all this had to have taken five to almost ten minutes before he backed up with his little camera to get the whole deer, his coat, and rifle in the picture.

In fact he had walked a little ways away and turned around, as he looked through the viewfinder of his camera he realized something did not look just right!

It appeared that his monster buck was no longer in the prone position! His trophy buck was now standing up shaking its head trying to figure out what was caught in and hanging from its antlers!

This was before his trophy buck decided to run off, with our (still too surprised to even take a picture with the camera he held), hunter's gun and jacket!

O' don't worry the jacket fell off as the buck went through the brush and another hunter did shoot this nice buck two days later running along through the woods with this deer rifle still laying across its antlers.

I never did ask him if he got a share of the deer seeing his rifle was attached to the deer the other hunter shot.

Nobody Told Me About This!

Now for the lighter side of deer hunting with the rest of the story you never seem to read about.

In the past in the *Fish Report* I told about the fun of watching a young hunter bag their first buck. There is nothing like it, but getting a deer is only half the fun for those involved. As this young hunter stands there admiring his first deer all of a sudden his whole life comes crashing down around him!

As he stands there one of the old timers gets out his hunting knife and states, "Now you get to clean your first buck!" Our young hunter had this one thought go back and forth through his mind, "They never showed or told about this part of deer hunting on all those outdoor shows he had watched."

This is when you need a video camera as our young hunter leans his gun against a tree, rolls up his sleeves, and gets ready as all the cheerleaders look on. You hear remarks like, "Make sure you don't get the knife in to far." "Watch out for the stomach" "Cut around it and just pull it out!" "Boy! Reach in there and grab a handful and just pull it out!"

Needless to say our young hunter does not seem to be enjoying this part of hunting as much as the older hunters turned cheerleaders seem too. But this is one of the things that go into hunting that for some reason there are those that are hunting for the first time never figured on.

But it gets even better when our young hunter gets home where he lives with just his mother. Now what do they do with his deer? Did anyone think of getting a rope to hang it up with? No! Is there any rope around the place? No! But they soon find the next best thing, the dog's chain. Now here is our young hunter with his mom and aunt trying to aid this young hunter hang his first buck up. This is when someone should have had a video camera from what I hear it was a comedy of errors. But they did manage to get it hung up. These are all the things that make up the education of a new deer hunter. There is no way you can ever replace the times had by all out there in the woods carrying on together. The time spent together can never be replaced and the people that take the time to take a young hunter out that lives with only his mother should be given a hardy "Thank You" from all of us.

Everybody should have a place where they can go and get away from all the problems of this day and age. This is my hideaway during a November deer season.

Chapter 3
Conservation Officer's Stories
Upper Michigan Tales from a Game Warden's Perspective
O'Man

No matter how hard a game warden tries there are always those days when life may have been better served if he had just rolled over and stayed in bed. But then you have to remember that what takes place on some of those days sure make for some interesting tales when the officers are sitting around in a hot tub after a meeting.

You just have to remember that being a game warden is something like hunting, you win some, you lose some and some end up in a tie. These are a few of those type days.

Gottcha!

Well, when spring and bad ice weather gets here, and when the fishing is at its best, and the seasons are closed on most species, this tale comes to mind.

It seems there was this game warden that just knew that this guy that spent 99% of his time hunting and fishing, without the interference of work, had a reputation of cleaning house on some of the small walleye lakes in the spring of the year when season was closed.

One day in early spring, when the ice was really bad, he received a tip that this guy was going to be fishing this river bend where there was a little bay for walleyes. Our game warden made plans to work the area so he could observe everything this party would be doing. In order to do this naturally he had to walk twice as far through the snow and mud that made up the way in at that time of year. He came in at the far side of the bay where there was a little rise so he could use his field glasses and watch out on the ice.

Sure enough, after he was about froze while waiting to see if anyone came into the area to fish, along came his "buddy". The ice was so bad that this fisherman had to use two pieces of plywood, moving one in front of the other, to work his way out on the ice. He finally got to an area out on the bay where he used his spud to make a number of holes through the ice, or should we say what was left of the ice. He finally got his gear out and started to fish. All this time being watched by the game warden.

Sure enough after a while he caught a few perch and then a real nice walleye, looked it over and then dropped it into the 5-gallon white bucket he had dragged out on the ice with him. A different one than he had been placing the perch in. During the course of the next hour and a half he caught three more nice walleye, placing each of these into the white bucket along with the first one.

Seeing by this time he was about froze solid and figuring he could come into where the party was fishing from his backside where the shore was closer our game warden made his move. Needless to say this was a white knuckle adventure for he too had to make his way out on the ice with a couple of boards seeing the ice was so thin. As quietly as he could he moved inch by inch up towards his quarry as the ice slowly moved up and down from his weight on it. Finally he was close enough to talk to the guy, watch the white bucket with the walleye in it, and finally catch this local poacher and quiet down all the talk about his fishing escapades in the local coffee shop.

He stood up on his board, ask the party for his fishing license and then ask him to hand him the white bucket. Case closed! Caught at last with at least four nice, out of season walleye! The game warden checked the license and then looked into the white bucket at the walleyes. Walleyes, walleyes! As he looked into the bucket in disbelief, all he saw was that the bucket did not have any bottom in it! In fact as he looked over, where the bucket had stood there was one of the holes the fisherman had made in the ice!

Can you believe this, risking your life, nearly freezing to death, while wasting a whole day, just to find that someone would go through all this work just to pull one on the game warden? It almost makes a game warden wonder who made that phone call leaving the tip in the first place?

Hold it! What's Wrong With This Picture?

There is a saying that goes like this, "What's wrong with this picture?" This is one of those tales that falls into this category.

It seems there was this game warden out on patrol working an area where he knew there was apt to be some illegal activity. He had been poking around for a while when he spotted a vehicle driven by one of the locals that was worth watching.

He kept an eye on the vehicle for a while and after satisfying himself that it was worth checking out he stopped the vehicle. The game warden got out and walked up to the vehicle and sure enough here was one of the local personalities driving it.

The game warden talked to him for a few minutes and during this time he shined his light into the vehicle and noticed a deer laying there. Needless to say it was not deer season at this time of year, a fact that mattered very little to a number of people that lived in the area where he worked. So he asked the party, "What are you doing with that deer in your vehicle?"

The party looked at the game warden and as serious as could be said, "I was driving around and saw this hurt deer laying on the edge of the road." He went on, "Seeing it was hurt and needed some help I decided to put it in my vehicle and take it to the vet, that's what I was doing when you stopped me, looking for the vet's office."

The officer looked at this "Good Samaritan" once again and then looked at the deer once again and had a real problem with this act of mercy in taking this hurt deer to the vet. You see one of the first things he had noticed when he first looked at the deer was the fact that the deer had already been gutted!

But I learned in college in some cases any answer is better than no answer at all, but not in this case.

The True Change In Women's Rights

The changes in times and those women that wanted to see equal rights for women has brought about one real change to the way things are done.

Back when I started you almost, in fact never, wrote a woman a ticket! You see she could fish free on her husbands fishing license so she was safe there. She could be standing at the stove cooking the illegally taken venison, but that was not her fault, she was just doing her duty in fixing supper. In fact one time we stopped a car with three illegal deer in it and only one person in it, the wife and mother of the crew. We went out and found the head of the clan and he was issued a ticket and took care of it without batting an eye. But boy have things changed now!

In fact the violator himself brought on a lot of the changes. As long as the decision was made out in the field about who was responsible and who was going to get the ticket everything was all right. It was all kept within the rules of "How things were done." You see mom could be part of the clan, but she was not the one responsible for supplying the food for the clan, dad was. Her job was just seeing it was fixed after the fact, and did this make her part of the illegal act.

But when the newer breed of violators started bringing things and excuses into the courtroom, did things change in a hurry. In no time at all mom had equal rights all right. Soon it did not matter who you wrote and if you wanted to you could write them both. O' but for the "Good, old, days".

I can recall times when the mom was cooking venison on the stove as you came over and still you only wrote the man of the house. Or if the husband and wife were both doing something illegal while snowmobiling etc, you only wrote the husband.

If the truth was known the people that received the break on the tickets helped to change the system so the wife had to receive a ticket also if she was involved by complaining to a judge at court.

Chapter 4

Conservation Officer's Stories
Upper Michigan Tales from a Game Warden's Perspective

So who's A Turkey?

You have to remember as you read any stories on turkeys that the main turkey hunting came well after I retired. There were a few turkeys in some of the areas where I worked, but nothing like there are today.

But, in order to sell a few of my books I have attended some of the biggest deer-turkey outdoor shows held in this country. Even if you are an old retired game warden for some reason people still like to come up and tell you their favorite story

Also in some cases what they tell you, when you hear it over and over, it sticks in your mind. The first part of this chapter will explain this to you and in some cases break your heart as you listen.

Dads Listen Before It's Too Late

During these shows you get to talk to both those with booths and those that attend the show looking to see the latest products or maybe look into a hunting trip somewhere.

One of the things that I have come to realize in the last few years is the tremendous growth in turkey hunting around the country. In fact in my opinion it has grown so much that there may come a day that turkey hunting will be equal to or have more participants than deer hunting does. I feel that one of the main reasons for this is the fact that the whole family can get involved in the sport all year around, indoors and out.

You ask how can this be when you only hunt turkey a few weeks out of the year? First of all they have clubs made up of those that like their turkey hunting, but not only this they have what amounts to a youth turkey hunting club where youngsters can get involved. When involved in these you can practice your turkey calling all year around. In fact I watched a dad trying to teach his six-year-old boy how to use a turkey call. The young lad was trying for all he was worth to get a sound out of his call that sounded something like dad's turkey call. This is the key and leads right into my next statement.

If I had one person come up to me to talk about my books I had a dozen come up and make this statement, "I still like my hunting, but I cannot get my boys involved in it no matter how hard I try". When you stop and think about it I guess this has to be one of the saddest statements a dad that loves to hunt and fish can make. I feel there are two reasons. The first you will understand, the second some of you may have to wear your seat belt when you read it to keep from going through the roof.

I think one of the reasons could be the fact that we went through an era where dad and his buddies did most of their hunting and fishing together. The hunting trips were planned around going with your buddies, not with putting up with your kids while trying to get a deer. Then all of a sudden the kids hit those teenage years and then dad tried to get them involved in hunting, but it was too late. The idea fell on unfertile ground.

This is why I think it is so important to have programs like the one for youth, even those not yet old enough to hunt, getting them involved in turkey hunting along with dad. In my books *Humans Are Nuts!* One of the things I talk about is getting your children involved and teaching them to like what you like. In a lot of cases the teenage years are too late. So get your children involved as young and as soon as you can in the great outdoors. If you are involved in a sportsmen's club make sure they have a youth program too, not just a time to go out and do some shooting and have a few drinks with the "boys".

The other thing is, and you better be ready for it and willing to fight it, is the fact that in a whole lot of cases there are public schools out there teaching your kids to be anti-hunting and anti-guns! You can say, "Not in my area!" But this is not true in a whole lot of cases.

Remember when parents were so worried about how so many things were subconsciously being taught to kids a few years back? Well the method has not gone away. If you teach youth that trees, animals, and birds have the same rights as humans what are you indirectly teaching them? If you teach youth that owning guns are wrong and those that own them are not the better people of our nation, what are you teaching them?

Remember if you don't spend time with your children teaching them to enjoy and respect the things you like to do, someday you may be just like this dad that stood in my booth last weekend and said, "I just cannot get my son involved in hunting with me now that he is old enough to go with me."

Was It Fowl Play Or A Suicide?

One story that was told to me was about a turkey that committed suicide. This happened a long time back, but the story is still told.

It seems that there was this turkey hunter out hunting all set up way before daylight. He was in his full camo sitting in a brush pile a little way off a fencerow with his turkey squawk box. After he made a few calls he got a reply from across the field. He worked on this turkey and got it to work its way across the field and then along the fencerow. When he got a good look at it he could see it was a nice male with a nice looking beard.

He kept up his calling and watched as his turkey was slowly getting into range. Just a little farther along the fence row and he could get a good shot. There were places along this fencerow where there were patches of brush and places where brush had been laid against the fence post. Here came his turkey strutting along the fencerow returning his calls from his squawk box, just a little more. Now he was in range. He passed through this place where there was some brush along the fence row and at this time the hunter got his shotgun all ready to make a good head shot.

The turkey strutted along and just when our hunter was going to shoot he ducked behind some brush on the fencerow. Our hunter kept his shotgun aimed at the spot where the turkey had ducked its head and waited for his head to pop up again. When it did our hunter pulled the trigger and the head disappeared behind the brush pile once again.

Our hunter ran over to the fencerow and brush pile to claim his prize turkey. As he reached down and picked it up he received a real surprise! Here lay not his prize turkey that he had watched for almost an hour all the way across the field and down the fencerow, but a hen turkey! Where had it come from? He had only saw the one turkey, a male, where had this hen come from? But better yet where had the turkey he had been watching disappear too? He never saw it leave the area even after he shot. Sometimes life takes some interesting twists.

An Out & Out Homicide!

It seems that there was this hunter that lived in an area where if you did not always carry a gun in your pickup truck you just felt that you left home partly undressed. On this day this was not so.

As our party drove down a 4-lane, now you can bet he was not up here in Yooperland, road that was not an expressway he saw a flock of turkeys run across the road up in front of him. He stepped on the gas and got up to where they cross the road and spotted them off to his left. Being the naturalist he was he stopped to watch them.

It seems that this flock of turkeys had run across the road and came up to one of those woven wire fences that run along the highways in a lot of areas. Needless to say the turkeys could not get through the fence and were to close to fly over it. So they would just run his way and then back the other way trying to get through the fence. Every once in a while one would try to fly over the fence only to hit it and drop back to the ground.

Our concerned citizen really got worried as he watched them, and thinking they are going to hurt themselves trying to get to the other side of that fence. Being the type citizen he was, and having a shotgun in the truck with him, he decided to shoot one of the turkeys before it got hurt. So he got out shot one and threw it in the back of his truck and headed down the 4-lane for home.

As he drove down the 4-lane he all of a sudden realized that he was seeing something in the rear view mirror. As he turned around and looked in the back of his pickup here was his turkey jumping up and down trying to get into the air and leave!

Our humanitarian had a real problem seeing it would ruin his day to be observed driving down the road with a wild turkey jumping up and down in the back of his pickup seeing it was not really turkey season at this time of year. It could ruin his whole day and might be rather hard to explain.

So he slammed on his brakes, pulled over to the side of the road, jumped out of his pickup, and convinced his turkey passenger that it might be better if he rode under the spare tire the rest of the way home.

Could This Be True?

I have always been told that turkey hunting is harder than deer hunting. From what they tell me, and from the few times I have been out, turkey can be as weary as any type creature you can hunt.

It seems that they have a way of picking anything out that might not belong. It seems like this was explained to me when I brought my white Shell coffee cup on a turkey hunt with me. How was I to know?

It also seems they can tell which side of the road you can hunt on and where they can be safe from any activity. In fact, they are so sure they are safe in some cases they will drive the average turkey caller nuts answering his calls while strutting up and down just back in the woods on the safe side of the road.

In fact, turkey can tell what date it is too! It seems while sitting in my bow tree blind for a number of days in an area where I had never observed a turkey at all, the day after turkey season closed here came four of them walking by right under my tree!

They all, the four turkey that is, were not all that lucky though because obviously there were some deer hunters out there during the firearm deer season that could not tell a turkey from a deer. Two of them turned up missing by muzzle loading season in December.

It really bugs me when any person that calls themselves a sportsman has to shoot something just to feel he got something while out in the woods. After all the time I spent as a Game Warden, and what I heard later on and am still hearing your chances of getting caught are slim and none. Thank goodness 99% of the hunters and fishermen out there just love the outdoors and try to do things within the law.

This is the next generation of hunters coming up in the family. This is my son Rob, with a nice buck he shot, along with my grandson Jonathan.

Chapter 5
Conservation Officer's Stories **Upper Michigan Tales from a Game Warden's Perspective**
Godzilla

It can be totally amazing who a game warden can run into out there on his travels. In some cases one has to wonder just what he may have walked into. This tale is one of those cases.

Pretty Please?

On this early fall morning I had plans to be up way before daylight and head off to work near the wildlife refuge at Fish Point off Saginaw Bay.

The plans were to get there way before daylight so I could get into position to watch and see if anyone would try and get into an area where the ducks spent the night to try and ground swat them before they woke up and headed out to the farm fields right at daylight.

I got into my hiding place and watched a footpath where people would come from the road along a cornfield looking for ducks. Sure enough after I had been there a little while a couple of hunters moved along the path going into an area at the edge of the woods. I watched them check out a small pothole where there were a lot of ducks but they made no move to take any.

About ten minutes later two more hunters came down the path and unlike the first two got down and crept up on the pothole where the ducks were. They moved through the tall grass on the edge of the pond and when some ducks took off one of the men took a shot at them. It did not appear he hit anything, but it was still dark and a good thirty minutes before legal shooting hours.

I got up and walked up to the two men, told them who I was, and asked to see their hunting license. The party that had shot at the ducks stood up and right away I was amazed at the size of him. If it wasn't Godzilla himself, it sure was one of his close relatives.

After he finished standing up he told me where I could go and what his personal impression of me wanting to see his hunting license was. My first thought was, "And the day is only starting."

The second thing that went through my mind was the fact that he was standing there with a shotgun, was twice my size, and already told me in so many words to drop dead. I tried to convince him he really ought to give me his shotgun seeing he had broken a federal waterfowl law and we would talk things over. He was not impressed. So I decided to latch onto his shotgun along with him and see if he would change his mind. He didn't.

After we had danced around a little while out there in the duck marsh he decided to let me have the gun, but he still would not give me any ID. I gave him a choice, show me some ID and I will write you out a ticket or we will be off to the county jail. He flat told me to take him to jail so off we went.

When we got to the county jail I finally, with the aid of a deputy, convinced him that he was getting nowhere by not telling a law enforcement officer his name, by law he had too. Finally he did give us a name and birth date. While filling out the paperwork the deputy in the radio room ran a record check on the name and date of birth he had given us. We about died as the LEIN machine started printing this guy's criminal record! It kept going and going.

Finally I started reading it, and found safe jobs at night, robbery, drug thefts, drug store B&E's, on and on went all this guy had been active in.

Finally he asks to make a phone call that all people have a right to make when they are placed in jail. We dialed a number he gave us and he talked to a party about needing some money that he was in jail. No sooner did he hang up but the switchboard at the jail lit up and federal agencies started calling asking what we had this guy booked for?

Now you have to understand we figured that this party called a restaurant in the Detroit area with his one phone call and right away federal law enforcement agencies start calling the jail. What does this tell you? A wiretap on some big place they are interested in where they overheard my duck hunter talking? So here these elite law enforcement officers call and want to know right away what we have this guy booked for which they are interested in? A safe job Exspurt, a robber, an Exspurt at getting into closed places where drugs are at night, on and on, so they ask, "What have you got him in jail for?

So the game warden has to tell them what the big crime really was, "shooting at a duck thirty minutes before shooting hours!" Boy were they impressed.

Honest they really were, for you see to shoot at a duck thirty minutes before shooting hours you usually are in possession of a firearm and with his criminal record it was against federal law for him to have a firearm!

So the Feds took over and were happy to have something on our early waterfowl shooter.

Why'd I Say That?

As I have stated before it has always amazed me that the DNR of the state of Michigan does not have a way of running a record check to see if someone can legally posses a firearm before they sell him a hunting license, that is his permit to have a firearm out in the woods. But..

In the area where I was working there was this rocket scientist in disguise that was a known violator. This party was something else and made sure it was no secret what he thought about game laws.

He was the type guy you kept hearing these weird stories about. Like the time he was out coon hunting with some buddies and sent his boy up in the tree to shake the coons out and shot his boy out of the tree instead of a raccoon. (He only hit him in the hand.)

Then there was the time they were out cutting pulp on a cold winter day when lunchtime came around. They had some cold cuts, and buns, but they did not have a knife or anything to slice the buns with. So our rocket scientist convinced his buddy to hold the buns and he would slice them with the chain saw so they could make sandwiches.

Now this is the type poacher a game warden needs a $10,000 computer and all the other modern equipment to try and catch when they are out there after a deer at night.

On this night we were running down a power line without our headlights on when we saw a beam of a spotlight go across the sky down the power line in front of us. Now if you have ever tried driving down a road along a power line at night in the dark you are nuts like the rest of us that did it.

Ten thousand chuckholes and bumps later we came up behind this pickup truck. There were two guys in it with the passenger using a spotlight shining the woods looking for deer. We followed them for a ways and then turned on the headlights, blue light, and spotlights to pull them over. They were not overly impressed with all the lights behind them, but they did shut the spotlight off and took off down the power line.

We followed them until they came to a two-track road and could see them using a CB in the cab of the pickup. Finally we came to an area where we could pull around them and stop them where there was a one lane bridge. In the truck we found a single shot shotgun, some buckshot, and a spotlight. All the time I was writing the ticket they railed on us about the ticket and what they thought about our job, but we gave them their tickets and left.

About three days later I received a call from the county parole officer asking if I could come down to a parole violation hearing at the county jail. I lived right in town so I said "sure" and went down.

When I got there he informed me that one of his parolees came in to report and wanted to tell him about the crappie ticket he had gotten the night before from the game warden. So he told the parole officer that he and a friend had been out in the woods and he had a shotgun with him when the local game warden came up behind him and tried to stop him.

He went on to tell that he kept going and tried to get some friends on the CB to come out and help him without any luck. So he finally stopped.

There was a panel of people from the state and court probation office at the jail, where I was informed that they were going to have a hearing on the parole violations from the party that had been shining. The parole officer told what the party had told him and about all I could do was agree because he had told him just like it happened, all but the fact they had been shinning.

They ask the defendant if he had anything to say and he said nothing except he thought the tickets were kind of chicken.

The parole board left for a minute and then came back and gave the party 6-months back in Jackson prison for being in possession of a firearm and another 6-months for having a CB in his vehicle.

I figured it was one of the better sentences for shining deer I had seen, but I could not really feel sorry for him because he had talked himself into it with the parole officer while talking about the crappie ticket he had gotten.

A little side note: It seems that the owner of the house where this guy was living received a tax notice where his taxes had went up on the old farmhouse where his parents had lived. He called the county tax office and asked why the taxes had gone up so much on the old homestead? He was informed that now that people were living in the house and seeing it was now livable it was worth more. His reply was, "Someone lives in the house?" It seems our parolee had just drove around until he found an empty house and moved himself and his family in. They had been living there for two years before he was caught.

Now I ask you, do you really think that a modern Conservation Officer needs a $10,000 computer, a car radio and phone, and all the modern goodies to catch someone with this frame of mind?

28

This is what you call a real Yooper deer blind that has to be almost Game Warden proof. In fact is it a blind or a house?
(Someone sent me this on my E-mail)

Chapter 6

Conservation Officer's Stories
Upper Michigan Tales from a Game Warden's Perspective

Goofs

Well, needless to say nobody likes to admit it when they goof up and blow a real good case on someone they have been trying to catch for a long time, but it does happen. I guess it takes more of a person to admit things did not work out just like they should have than the person that tries to railroad someone without the evidence. Here are a few stories along this line.

I Thought You Had It?

One time I was working with one of the veteran officers on some Spring pike runs. We were working an area where we knew there were a lot of pike and had heard they were a few being removed for lunch. We had come into the area after dark, hid the patrol car and walked a long ways back into the spawning area to hide and wait.

After we had been sitting in the bushes for a while we heard some people coming through the woods. We waited and after a little while we saw some flashlights being used down in the creek in the area where the pike usually spawn.

All of a sudden we could tell by their excitement that they had managed to see some nice ones. They went back into the woods to find a small sapling to use for a spear handle and returned to the creek. A short time later we saw the lights make a rush for the bank and place something in a gunny sack. They seemed to have pretty good success at least twice more before we managed to sneak up on the creek and get behind them.

You have to remember you have to get within grabbing distance before you can make a sound or let them know you are there or else all you will have for all your waiting and trouble will be the smell of burnt rubber as they take off through the woods running.

So we got right behind them and made our catch for the night.

There were three of them and they had a gunny sack with at least three nice pike in it. We got some ID from them, picked up the sack of fish, and started our long walk back to the road and the patrol car. They told us where their car was so one of us walked out with them while the other officer went to get the patrol car and drive down to where they were. The one walking out with the spears took the sack of fish with him.

We had just arrived at their car when the patrol unit pulled up and stopped right behind their car. I walked to the back of the patrol car, dumped the sack of fish out and counted them and then placed them back in the sack.

The other officer sat in the patrol car and wrote out tickets for the three subjects for spearing pike out of season. The spears, with their long handles were placed in the back seat and we took off happy as could be for the crew we had caught that evening after all the time and planning it took to get them.

We were riding around about a half-hour later when a light seemed to go on and someone asked, "How did you get that sack of fish into the trunk?" AWWWWWWWW!

You see back in those days you did not have that little button inside the car to open the trunk with; you had to use a key. And the key was in the ignition because the car was running while the other officer was sitting in the car to write out the tickets.

We turned around and made tracks back to where we had parked to write out the tickets, but needless to say the poachers, their vehicle, and the sack of pike were no longer there.

So with the key evidence for the case gone there was only one thing we could do, bite the bullet and drop the charges on the three. You may ask, "But you still had the spears why not charge them for these?" Well, we could have if it had been a trout stream, but we were not even lucky enough for this to be true, so we had nothing.

So we had two choices, either we could tell the story and laugh about how things had gone or we could cry and grown men are not supposed to cry.

We Needed Just A Little Bit Of Something

One night we were out working shiners and had been running around up north near Stuben without using any headlights when we saw a vehicle coming north on M-94. We pulled into a two-track and waited to see what the vehicle was up to seeing it was well after midnight.

The vehicle came to the road that goes into Stuben, which at the time was a gravel road and turned toward the west and headed down the road. We pulled onto the road and pulled in right behind this late night car to see what they were up too.

They went right by Stuben and headed into an area where most of the houses were summer homes so late night travel was not too common. This car we were behind was going real, real slow and once in a while it would swing from side to side so its headlights would shine off into the woods or any open area where there might be deer.

After following them for over and hour we were coming down Thunder Lake Road heading into the Cooks area. We figured we had better pull them over seeing it was obvious they had been looking for deer with their headlights all the way through the back-woods area on this gravel road. I turned on the blue-light, head-lights, and spotlights to pull the vehicle over. They went only a lit-tle ways down the road and pulled over.

We walked up and there were two people in the car, both were rid-ing in the front seat, there was no one riding in the back seat. When we had them get out of the car and looked in the car we saw a shotgun inside the car. There was also a flashlight, but we had not seen this being used.

We asked the two people to step between the patrol car and their car while the inside of their vehicle was checked out good. We did not find any shells for the shotgun. While asking for some ID from the two people I noticed that the driver had an object in his pocket that looked to be about the size of a box that you would buy slugs in. I ask him if I could see what he had in his pocket and he said, "sure."

He reached into his shirt pocket and to my surprise handed me a small metal Band Aid box. I took it and opened it and said, "Mmm, What's this?"

He let out a yelp and then yelled, "Give me that back!" and made a grab for it. I kept it because when he had handed it to me without thinking and I had opened it up I saw it was full of marijuana! It must have slipped his mind when he handed it to me.

Now we had the shotgun, and watched them trying to find deer with their headlights, and a Band Aid box full of marijuana. Things were looking up and really improved when the driver being fed up with what he had just done reached into his pocket and handed me some slugs for the shotgun.

After we had written them tickets for the violations we took the evidence and called it a night. The marijuana was sent to the state police crime lab to be tested to prove it was what it really was and everything turned out great. To top things off this was about the fifth time I had caught the one party for night hunting or this type violation. We were ready for court, because you could count on them pleading, Not Guilty.

The day for the trail came up and we had our game plan figured out to a tee. Everything went as planned and everything fell into place just like they were supposed to. The crime lab officer was there with his report where our Band Aid box proved to have been filled with marijuana.

Man, we were on a roll! Until the prosecutor ask the man if he had the Band Aid box with the marijuana in it with him? Right away by the look on his face I knew we were in trouble! He had the report, the expertise, everything but the physical evidence we needed.

There was really nothing we could do about it, the lab was too far away, and court was already well along. It was just one of those things we all have done, thought of everything but the most important thing.

So when the prosecutor gave his closing argument to the jury he did everything but include the charge for possession of marijuana. The only charge they had to come to a conclusion about was whether they had been head lighting deer or not.

After being out for just a short time the jury returned and they had found both subjects guilty of trying to locate deer with the aid of an artificial light while in the possession of a firearm.

When I walked out of the courthouse after everything was over there were a couple of the people that had been on the jury waiting for me. They were a little upset about the fact they had not been able to find the party guilty of possession of marijuana after the evidence was so cut and dried that he had it in his shirt pocket.

I tried to explain to them the legal reason the way things had went the way they did. Even after this they informed me, "We don't care he had it and we would have found him guilty anyway!"

But that's life.

Two special people in my life
Sue and Howard Strasler

Chapter 7
Conservation Officer's Stories   **Upper Michigan Tales from a Game Warden's Perspective**
True Friends

Some of the best advice I was taught in growing up was to learn to have a few good people you could call on for advice when you needed it. I took this advice to heart and even after my Dad was no longer around to give me advice and help when I needed it there were always a couple of men I could count on.

When the family and I moved to Manistique there were two other families that came to town about the same time we did. One was returning home while the other came here as a businessman. They were both real successful in their endeavors and were always willing to listen to me and offer suggestions.

Howard Strasler owned Sunny Shores Restaurant on US-2 here in Manistique. We became real good friends and one important thing I learned from Howard that I **try** to live by is that he never had a bad day.

I could stop to talk to him when weather was lousy and there were no tourist moving around, they were the key to his restaurant business, so he and I would be the only two people in the whole place having a cup of coffee. Needless to say this was not paying the bills! I would ask Howard, "How has business been?" He would never in all the years I knew him and all the times I ask him say that he was having a bad day. In Howard's mind it may not be a good day, but it still was never a bad day. What a lesson I learned.

I don't know how many times when I started out doing my books I would go and talk to Howard about what he thought. I can still recall and be so thankful for his advice. One piece of advice he told me was, "John be willing to sell one or two books to any business that wants only one or two. If you sell one book a dozen times or a dozen books once, you still sold a dozen books." Some of the best advice I had.

One time I got this bright idea and thought it would be just great to go along with my books. I went out and talked it over with Howard and he maybe wanted to, but never came out and told me it was a dumb idea. He made me a suggestion and even helped me see if my idea would work with it only costing me twenty cents instead of hundreds of dollars. Needless to say my great idea was only worth twenty cents and not all that was profit.

Howard never came back and made you feel like maybe you should have felt after falling on your face, he was only thankful you were willing to ask him and accept his advice. Needless to say I was too.

I could give you a whole list of suggestions Howard gave me and believe it or not they always were helpful to me. People ask me all the time how I ever managed the success with my books and one of the keys was being willing to listen to people trying to help.

Needless to say sitting here working on book number seven there is no longer a "right-hand-man" to get advice from anymore and I sure miss the friendship and honest advice he was always willing to give me.

A Yooper Helps Out

I have never told this story about Howard and I am now telling it like I remember it after all these years because after telling me it he never mentioned it again. That was the type person he was. Please remember this is how I recall this story.

Howard and Sue were down south during the winter a number of years back visiting her parents. It was a nice warm sunny morning as they drove along the highway together talking and not paying much attention to anything.

Howard mentioned to Sue that there was a police vehicle parked up ahead on the highway with its lights flashing. (You have to understand that Sue's father was a retired police officer so for some reason having grown up in a law enforcement officer's home you always seem to show more interest when seeing a patrol car stopping someone.)

Howard pulled over in the inside lane and went to go past the patrol car and the vehicle they had stopped. Just as he went to pass the patrol car an officer flew out from between the cars to sprawl out on the road. Without thinking seeing the officer was obviously hurt, Howard pulled into the meridian and stopped putting on his 4-way flashers. When the vehicle that had been stopped by the officer saw this it took off down the highway.

Howard went back to the patrol car and seeing the officer was hurt got on the police radio and asked for help. Needless to say help came in a hurry. The fleeing car was later stopped and the party arrested.

I ask Howard if he ever even thought what might have happened to Sue and him seeing a police officer had already been hurt? He told me, NO, I did not even take time to think, I only knew an officer was hurt and I should stop and help.

He did tell me that after thinking about it he was glad he had a car at the time that when you turned on the 4-way flashers they flashed in the rear window. He also said when he did this and he got out with a white, short sleeve shirt and dress slacks that maybe the person in the car thought he was a detective in a unmarked police car.

I don't know how many people knew this story about Howard, but it kind of tells where his heart was in helping out other people.

No Greater Love

Well, there are just some times in life when things just seem to narrow down to what really is important. When these times come for some reason I do not feel like doing a normal Fish Report. You do not feel like it is too important if the fish are hitting and you sure do not feel like writing about one of the humorous things that happened. For some reason that big, hurting, empty feeling in the pit of your stomach hurts too much.

Sometimes in life even with all the modern technology we have a person can feel so helpless it just hurts. This is one of those times.

Sunday evening when we returned home, after spending the weekend down at my boy's, and were coming into the city limits, I just had this funny feeling about things. It's strange, but sometimes you just feel like something is just not right. I had only been home a short time when the phone rang and someone called and told me about the missing hunters Marvin Grover and his grandson Jeff Zellner up in the High Roll-A-Ways. I called some of the family to see what was going on, and then called my kids to tell them about it and ask them to pray about things.

Back at least a zillion years ago now when we moved to Manistique there were two other families that came to town about the same time. There were Sue and Howard Strasler and Marvin and Marie Grover with their families. For some reason I got to be friends with both these families and nobody will ever understand how often they helped me out along with my family in the years to come. I cannot count all the times when some of the biggest decisions of life came along that I went and called on one of these two men to consult with. Friends can do this even if like in my case it was usually a one-way street; I could receive some good advice, but maybe came up short in what I could give in return.

You see friendships are something that we will never really understand and should always value and treat with special care. This I was reminded of once again in the last couple of days. When I started writing the Fish Report so many years ago I always tried to put the value of the camaraderie of hunting in the stories about hunting and fishing with your buddies.

When I called my boy down in Wisconsin I ask him to call one of Marvin and Jeff's hunting buddies that now lives down there. My boy called back a few minutes later and said that this buddy and his dad (that was down for the weekend) were already on their way north. Overnight there were hunting buddies and family friends coming from all over the U.P., Lower Michigan and Wisconsin. There were even hunting buddies from as far away as Ohio making the trip north to see if they could help out.

Along with these were all the friends from around the area that were calling or arriving to see if they could be of some help. There were people on 4-wheelers checking every camp, trail and possibility they could think of. There were people with their 4-wheel drive vehicles hitting all the back roads on both sides of the river to try and locate the two missing hunters. All the different law enforcement agencies from the area were working as a team to try and make things work in an almost impossible situation with the weather.

In a lot of cases it was not only their job and their responsibility, but out of the friendship and respect that had been built up through the years that now was returning ten-fold from all these people when the need arose. People from all walks of life and all backgrounds were either there or calling to see if they could be of any help.

You see if there was ever a case where the term "sportsman" applied it would be in this case with Marvin and the enjoyment he had running his dogs.

As I write this Fish Report the search is still going on and all these friends of the two missing hunters are still out there looking and hoping for some sign of the two. But no matter what happens the bond of friendships that were built through years of enjoying the great outdoors while running their dogs is something that leaves even more respect for these two men as you watch the faces of those searching for them.

As the old saying goes, "Some things money cannot buy" and true friendships are one of those.

One of the other men that was always willing to take time to help me out was Marvin. Sitting here writing about these two men I have to wonder what they really thought at times when I talked to them. But I will always be thankful for the down to earth way these two men were and the way they helped me out. This and the following article are two I wrote in the *Fish Report* about Marvin.

The Other Side I Knew Of Marvin

If you have read enough of my articles and any of my books you know that I try to portray that there is more to hunting and fishing than measuring it only by what you manage to take. I have always tried to tell the stories I write with the emphasis on the friendships you make and the fun people have getting together on their trips to the great outdoors. In the last month in my travels to outdoor shows and art festivals with my books this fact has hit home all the more in talking to people. If I had one person say that I should write about what I am going to write I had dozens say this. Friends, relatives, and business acquaintances all ask if sometime I could do this. I really did not know what would be appropriate, but I thought with the benefit dinner coming up on the 11th this might be a good time.

You see when all the articles were written about Marvin Grover on account of what took place they were all centered around his love for running his dogs and hunting, but as I have told so many people this was a small part of why so many people liked him. You see most of us never went running dogs or hunting with Marvin, so this was not what made him special, it was his smile and character we learned to love.

It was the dozens and dozens of times that some young person from town was trying to earn money to go on a youth outing or to camp that Marvin, (and when I say Marvin I also mean to include his wife), came through. He would call me up or see me on the street and ask if any of the youth needed some help? Then he would give them some work to do because he thought it would help build their character if they earned the trip by working for it. But then Marvin being Marvin he would usually pay them way more than the job was worth just because he wanted to help them out.

It was the time a young Conservation Officer, new in town, was looking for a house when houses for sale were hard to find in Manistique. He finally found one he could afford and made an agreement with the older lady that owned it to purchase it. In fact he ask Marvin for some advice, which he gladly gave to him. Only a couple of years later did he find out that Marvin really had the house listed. The older lady never knew she was not suppose to sell it after it was listed and the young Conservation Officer and his family needed a home so he never said a word, even if it did cost him his commission.

It was the call I would get once in a while on a Monday morning from Marvin asking me if I was going to be busy at noon. I don't know if he was scraping the bottom of the barrel and hit the W's and found Walker or what, but it seemed he was in charge of the program for his noon luncheon get together and needed some help quick, and could I bail him out!

It was the man that would give me a call to say he needed a couple dozen of my books. You see when a father and son would come into the office to talk to him about some property he liked to have the boy leave with one of the books so he could enjoy it and see what we were like up here in God's Country.

I could go on and on with stories about why so many people like Marvin and Marie, but space would not allow for it. But so many of his friends asked me if I could take the time to let you see the other side of Marvin that they knew. Hopefully this will give you a glimpse of his character and why so many people feel like they do outside of hunting.

Needless to say I miss these two men and for some reason a person feels a little older each time they see people around their age moving on to that perfect deer blind in the sky.

But I will be eternally thankful for all their help and the friendships we enjoyed. This is also what makes living in a place like Michigan's U.P. something special.

Marv and his grandson Jeff

Chapter 8

Conservation Officer's Stories
Upper Michigan Tales from a Game Warden's Perspective

Some Of The Most Interesting People I Have Met

One thing I would have to admit is with the job I had I sure came across and had a chance to meet some real interesting people. Some were people that just jumped off and took off to do something they always wanted to do with their life. There were others that grew up without any respect for the rules in the great outdoors, but as life went on they seemed to take a real interest in the great outdoors. Here are a few short stories about some of these people.

I Could Bearly Believe It

I can remember plain as can be the first time I ever heard about this party. He had worked down in the Bay City area as a fireman and when it came time to retire he packed his bags and moved to the great north woods north of Newberry.

This man had been involved for years with some rather interesting projects, one of these being running a tough man contest. Needless to say he was a rather large man and tough as nails.

One day one of the officers that worked for me came into the District Office and told me that he had to take a ride north of Newberry and have a talk with Dean Oswald again. I ask him what for because I had never heard of this party before.

John told me that Dean was misbehaving with his pet bear again. I thought, "Run that by me once again, trouble with his pet bear?"

So John told me that Dean Oswald had a permit for having a pet bear and he seemed to enjoy getting the tourist attention with it. It seems that Dean was misbehaving again by bringing his bear to town. (Maybe someone should have wrote a song titled, *Don't take your bear to town Dean, leave your bear at home."*)

Here would come Dean into town in his pickup truck and who

would be sitting there riding in the passenger seat? Here would sit his pet bear big enough to get any poor Trolls attention as they were vacationing in the Newberry area.

Here he would come down the main street of Newberry with his bear, pull into a parking spot and get out and walk down the sidewalk with his bear into wherever he was going. Needless to say there were those that were not impressed with a bear walking down the sidewalk in their town. Others just laughed knowing Dean.

So the officer would go out and talk to Dean and things would settle down for a little while. Dean decided that he enjoyed being around his bear so much that he started a place to breed and raise bear.

Now I ask you, how many people do you know that would retire and then go out and start a ranch raising black bear? Just maybe an x-marine? I have no idea how many bear are at his place now, but there are a lot of them.

I guess with my nature I have always respected a person that had a dream, and no matter how crazy it may seem to other people, would just go out and make his dream come true. This is what this man did.

Then again even before I ever heard of Dean I always thought it would be neat to have a large bear for a VCO. Needless to say most people you ran into out there would think twice before giving an officer a hard time if he had a bear on patrol with him. So maybe Dean and I had something in common, only he was crazy enough to do more than just think about it.

Now if you get up in the U.P. near the Newberry area you will have to make that trip three miles north, take a left and go see Dean and his bear ranch. There is nothing like it and you will always remember seeing this many black bear when they are so hard to see out in the woods.

This is one of the few places where I see people of all ages and walks of life with an amazing look on their face as they watch Dean's bear.

From A Poacher To A Preacher

I guess when you are a Game Warden you are bound to run into areas where you have to wonder about some of the friends that come along. In the case of this man chances of him ever becoming a real friend of the Game Warden were slim and none! In fact he could probably tell more interesting Game Warden stories than I could.

The story below is just as it was read and told at his funeral service after he was killed when a car hit him while riding his motorcycle. I guess in my opinion this man's example is one of the best how a person should live a Christian life. Always doing things for others, and never asking anything in return.

As you travel the road of life you may have many friends, but you usually have only a few real friends. These are the ones that are always doing something for you while never asking or even expecting anything in return. Brother Gerald was one of these.

It seems like so long ago that a number of us would travel over to Bark River, go north a little ways, to the Viau's house. Brother Gerald had really just been led to the saving knowledge of Jesus Christ a short time before. But, if anybody ever got 100% saved and truly felt sure of what he was to do for the Lord, Brother Viau sure knew. (We could almost call this, *From a Poacher to a Preacher*) He knew God had called him to be a preacher almost from the time he decided to give his life to Him, there was never a doubt in his mind. Many times when a lesser man would have folded his tent and quit, he just kept on going for the Lord.

I always felt it was one of the biggest honors I ever had in my Christian life when I was asked to sit on the ordination board for Brother Gerald. You have to understand God's humor when He would allow a Game Warden to be part of Brother Viau's service. Here was a man from the backwoods of Michigan's U.P., without any college training, without the support of a home church, or any organization to support him, going from a poacher to a preacher, just stepping off to serve his Lord and Savior. The people on the board asked Brother Gerald a number of questions and all felt we were impressed by his faith and his heartfelt calling from the Lord. We were all more than glad to recommend Brother Gerald be ordained as a preacher of God's Word. He surely more than fulfilled what was expected of him.

The love Brother Gerald had for the people up here in the backwoods maybe came from his ability to relate to how some of them lived. The example of his life showed how a person can be an example for young people from the changes in his life. No matter what he never quit!

I could fill the rest of this book just telling tales of the battles he fought. There were those that tried to wreck his church and testimony, but he kept on. There had to be times when the battle made him weary, his wife may have saw him when he was down, but we never did. Did he ever wonder if the life of a poacher was a whole lot easier than that of a preacher? I can still sit here and remember his crocked little smile, and that truly caring look for others that was always in his eyes. He knew what the Lord wanted him to do and nobody on earth was going to stop him from doing it.

This is why I had Brother Gerald, past truck driver, construction worker, yes and even a poacher, speak at a number of my youth banquets when I worked with the youth at my church. If you really knew me, you would know that I feel and have always felt that true character is the true key to fulfilling God's will in your life. I wanted the youth from Bethel Baptist Church to see this in Brother Viau.

As I said at the start, Brother Gerald always thought of and helped others as he felt our Lord surely did. Even after getting burned and the short end of the stick so many times, he still kept on doing what he felt was right. When a normal person would have finally gotten tired and quit, Brother Gerald just kept on going and never did.

Here are a couple of examples of Brother Viau's caring:

He would work all day and then drive all the way over to Manistique to bring a number of youth to attend our youth group's activity because his church was not big enough to have an activity at the time. He would then just sit around for two-three hours while his youth took part in the activity and then drive them all the way back home. Sometimes this could be a four-five hour evening and then he would have to get up early the next morning for Sunday's services.

Always letting me call him at the last minute, when taking a crew of youth to the Bill Rice Ranch down in Murfreesboro, TN, to ask if I could borrow his bus when too many youth signed up for the trip to take our church van. In fact a number of times he made the trip with us. I always felt he was there if I ever needed him and he always was.

Whenever he saw needs in the rest of us, both spiritually and otherwise, he would just step forward and offer his help. One night when he had brought his youth over to our activity we got talking about my books. I told him I had just written another book and was having trouble finding a way to get the shipment from Springfield, MO to Michigan. A couple of days later I received a call from Brother Viau telling me he had made a couple of phone calls and a trucker would pick up my books in Missouri for me and was taking them to the Manistique Paper Mill where I could pick them up. It was a small thing, and little in the eyes of the world, but it showed how he cared about people and liked to help them out. I had never ask or suggested he help me, it was just his way.

Brother Gerald loved his wife and family. When his wife was so sick one winter, he was a godly husband staying by and caring for her. With the battles of life all of us parents go through, Brother Gerald was there for his kids. He had fun with them, cried with them, and hurt with them being what a godly father should be. When some of us, that were saved later in life, have family members that do not always understand the change in ones life, the what or why of what you are doing, Brother Gerald stilled loved and cared for his family as a true Christian should. He was this way right up to the end.

Brother Gerald was typical of the backwoods preachers that for years made their way around our country and made it what it was for so many years. We could use a few down to earth, godly men like him in our country today.

Now here I sit, with that rock, that earthly stone, that true friend, that was always there, that I could depend on if I ever needed something, being gone.

But as I told Wifee, Brother Gerald is now sitting in the front row. If they gave out Gold Medals in heaven, Brother Gerald would be

Blame Her, The Fish Report Was Her Fault

You know it was over twenty years ago when I started writing the *Fish Report* for the Manistique Pioneer Tribune. Even then Leanne thought I was nuts in more ways than one. Now after all these years of the weekly *Fish Report* there is no longer any doubt in her mind.

The first time I can remember talking to Leanne was at the State Police Post where Lt. Bolt and I used to give her such a hard time about her little, small town newspaper. I can recall one time when we all got going about something that had been in the newspaper. So a short time after Leanne left flowers were dropped off at the post as a peace offering.

It's funny thinking back over all these years and all the long talks we had together about almost anything and everything. It is totally amazing that two people that may have two totally different philosophies about so many things in life still find out how many things they agree about. There are certain things Leanne will always be wrong about, but there just may be one or two things she may still think I am out in *"Right"* field about.

For a lady, that I am not sure we ever made a *"True, Blue, Yooper"* out of, she sure loved our little town and felt the importance of a small town newspaper. In an era when so many weekly newspaper were being bought up by the larger newspapers this bothered her. This and the fact that she never wanted **"her"** newspaper to become a supermarket tabloid-type newspaper. She did not believe it really helped anyone if the whole front page was covered with gut, gore, and crime.

And her paper never was. She felt her paper should show the positive side of things that happened in our little town. Besides you would have already heard all the gory things at coffee long before a weekly newspaper ever came out, so it was already history.

As I sit here and laugh to recall some of the letters she received about my *Fish Reports* from people that were edumacated.

Leanne understood the way I write things and how I express things is not the way a normal English Literature class would. It was never meant to be. It was just a Yooper's way of telling tales and having fun.

When I first started putting book number one *(A Deer Gets Revenge)* together, Leanne gave me some advice that proved to be what caused my books to sell the way they have. She said, *"John, don't let anyone correct the way you tell your stories out of your book. This is what people that read your stories like about them."* I took her advice and the Lord blessed me for being willing to listen to someone trying to help me out.

Nobody knows how hard it is even to write a little, silly book like mine unless they are involved in this type of work. I can say Leanne understood when I would go in and show her something and ask her advice about it. I will have to say I was crushed one time when she told me, *"John, when you told me you had ordered 5,000 copies of your first book, for an unknown author from the middle of nowhere I thought you were nuts! But, you sounded so positive about it, I never said a word."* Maybe it's a good thing or she may have scared me into an early grave.

Changes always come along as we go through life, but some of them we hate to see because of the friends that are involved. Leanne always enjoyed hearing about the scholarship fund from my book sales and about people that called about my books. For this reason I will close with this little story.

Last week a lady called from Flint, MI and wanted to order two copies of *A Deer Gets Revenge.* She also wanted to tell me this story about her dad. Dad had been in the hospital with heart problems and things had not gone well. It seems that he was in and out of the hospital three times with surgery and all. The third time he came home he had about given up and would only sit in his chair. Her dad would not eat, watch TV or anything.

It seems that when she had been up north she had purchased my book *A Deer Gets Revenge*, so she gave it to her dad to read hoping it would cheer him up. She said he had always been an avid hunter and fishermen, so when he started to read the book he read it from start to finish. Dad got a kick out of the book and started to eat with the family again and enjoy things like in the past.

She told me that her dad never fully recovered, but the last couple of days were spent with the dad they had always known. She said after he passed away, mom kept my book that had been such a help during their struggle with dad and would not give it back. This is why she was calling to order a couple of copies and to tell us this story.

See Leanne you were right once again. Thank you for all your help and being a friend in the true meaning of the word.

I will close with this piece of Yooper wisdom. I have always said, being a normal, red blooded, male, Yooper, that you really had respect for two types of people. *"First there are those that could beat the fire out of you. It was either respect them or die during recess. And then there were those that proved to be a whole lot smarter than you were or ever hoped to be, so you respected them for this."* And I hope Leanne does not plan on whipping me.

Chapter 9
Conservation Officer's Stories   **Upper Michigan Tales from a Game Warden's Perspective**
Some Quirky Short Adventures

In the adventures of life and working as a Game Warden there are always those things that come up that make life interesting. Some of them are things where maybe you should take a step back and think things over, but you are young and for some reason this never crosses your mind. Here are a few stories that fall into this area.

So That's The Thanks You Get

Back in the days when I first started out working as a game warden I was assigned down in the Thumb Area of Michigan at Caro.

One day while at the field office with my boss we received a call that a deer had went through the ice on the Cass River only a couple of miles from the field office. We got into our patrol car and went over to the area to see what we could do. After we arrived and walked down to the river we observed a medium size doe that had went through the ice. She could get her front feet up on the ice, but when she tried to get the rest of her body up on the ice it kept breaking away. It was apparent that her back feet were not touching bottom and the only thing keeping her from going under was her front feet and head being up on the edge of the ice. Now what?

After looking things over Jim (my boss at the time) radioed the field office and asked them to bring a long, large rope and some boards out to where we were. Now you have to consider this fact, if the ice was not strong enough to hold up a medium size doe there was no way it was going to hold up either one of us.

After the rope and the boards arrived Jim laid on his stomach and worked his way out to as close as he dare to where the deer was on the edge of the ice. By now the deer was in such bad shape that it just lay there and watched him creep out toward where she was.

When he got, as close to the edge as he could it was time for him to try his western skills. Now I have to admit that I have never observed a cowboy laying on his belly trying to throw a rope over a critter. Needless to say for a normal person to try and rope something outside the movies is bad enough; but from Jim's position it was even harder.

I cannot say how may times he tried before finally getting the rope over the deer's head and then worked his way back to shore. With a number of us pulling on the rope as the doe fought to get her back feet up on the ice we finally got her out.

She was in such bad shape that she made no attempt to leave, but just laid there on the ground after we got her to shore so we picked her up, placed her in a vehicle, and took her to the field office where she was put in the heated stall. The local vet came out to check her over. He said she should be all right that she was only cold and exhausted. So he gave her a shot and told us to just let her warm up.

A couple of hours later Jim opened the garage door to check on his patient and about got done in for all his effort. Here came our rescued doe across the garage, up on her hind feet trying to spear Jim with her front feet. Needless to say she had recovered fine so we went outside and opened the overhead door to let her out.

What did we receive for our rescue effort? Two things, first of all, our deer friend stayed around the field office long enough to eat all the ornamental cedar that were planted around the office right down to nothing. Then we received a letter from the Big House in Lansing recognizing our efforts in the rescue, but strongly suggested it may be better if one did not risk their life to rescue a deer in this manner again.

A Creature Of Habit

As I get writing some of these memories and the crazy things that take place up here in the north woods I always get thinking about Rocky. A man never had a better dog than he was and needless to say there are a lot of good memories.
Most of the time when the family went on vacation we took Rocky with us because after all he was a member of the family. Of course

there were a few times that he had to be left with someone because where we were going there just was not any place for him to stay.

On one of these occasions we returned home later in the evening and Cathy of course wanted to go out and pick up Rocky right away. After all the driving we had done that day I talked her into waiting until the next morning and promised we would go and get him first thing.

We went out to where he was staying and right away we knew something was wrong when he didn't come out to meet us when the people who were watching him opened the door of their house.

At this time Rocky was getting up in age and we figured maybe something had happened to him, but this was not the case. We were told that the lady that was watching him had let him out for just a minute and when she went to let him back in no Rocky. They had looked all over the area and could not find a trace of him.

Needless to say Dad was between a rock and a hard spot because if he had picked him up the night before like Cathy wanted he would have been at home already.

We covered the whole neighborhood looking for any sign of him, nothing. We even went house to house and ask the people living there if they had seen anything of a large, golden, retriever? Nothing. We called the State Police and the County Sheriff Department to see if anyone had reported him? Nothing. We were about at the end of our rope and were looking for any idea anyone may have when someone asked if we had called the radio station to see if anyone had reported finding a Golden Retriever? We had not so we called them right away.

They told us that a party that lived on Big Springs Road had called in and reported they had found a dog that fit Rocky's description that morning way up near Thunder Lake. This was hard to believe that he may have covered all that area, but we had nothing to lose in checking things out. So off we went with little hope, but maybe.

We got to the house on Big Springs Road and sure enough here came Rocky as fast as his old body could make it when he saw us.

Needless to say he had covered a lot of ground since the lady let him out of the house that morning. But we were sure glad to find him.

The only thing I have ever been able to figure out is that for some reason, in his old age when he was let out, he must have got thinking about all the times we had spent waterfowl hunting up in the Thunder Lake area and just figured we must be up there because he had not seen us for so long.

It is totally amazing how many miles this old dog traveled just to get to the area where we had so many great times together. It sure makes one wonder what can go through a dog's mind at times, but thank goodness we found him and Dad was off the hook once again.

Ask An Incriminating Question

There are always those times as Game Warden when you are just a little too early or a couple of minutes to late to see the person doing what would give you the evidence for an open and shut case. This happens more often than an officer would like to admit. When this does happen once again an officer has to go to plan B hoping to find out what happened.

On this evening we had received a complaint that someone was shining for deer out in the area of the Thompson Plains. We headed out that way and there was also a state police car close that heard the complaint.

By the time we got there the state police had a vehicle pulled over that was coming out of the area where the report of shining had come from. There were two people in the vehicle along with some firearms and other hunting equipment. Both the state police and the game wardens knew both of the subjects because they had been caught at least a dozen times before.

After talking to the state police we found that they had not really observed the parties in the vehicle use the spotlight they had in the car, but had watched them come out of the two-track road from back in a pine plantation. So here we were with two good subjects, all the equipment they needed to do a little night hunting, but with nothing really to tie it all together.

Now you have to understand that if the Game Warden walked up and asked them, "Were you shining for deer back there?" Chances are about 100% that he would get only one answer, "NO!" So like I said we had to come into the problem through the back door.

I had noticed one other object in the vehicle when I had walked up to it and this was a bait bucket. I knew that the people in the car hunted in this area during the firearm deer season. Also seeing it was deer season they could have the firearms in the car, but not if they were trying to locate deer with an artificial light.

So when I walked up to the driver's side window I asked the driver, "You know you can't use a spotlight to look for deer even if you are back there dumping bait don't you?" They told me they didn't know that and by using this question I got them talking about what they had been doing back there before we arrived.

Before they quit talking they had told us what they were doing, what they had tried to do, and even a few things we had no idea they were up too.

It is totally amazing how willing someone can be to tell you what is going on **"if"** you can use the right question to get him talking.

If they stopped and thought a minute they would remember that nobody that is a native of the U.P. ever uses the front door. Everybody up here uses the back door so they can clean the snow off their feet before going into the house. Maybe this is why a Game Warden sometimes gets the best results by coming in through the back door to get what he wants.

56

Pioneer Tribune

Walker's scholarship donations top $20,000
Success of books continues to amaze local author

"It has been totally amazing."

That's what Sgt. John Walker of Manistique says about his ongoing success as a self-published author. There are now 60,000 copies of his books in print. They are sold all over the country in a variety of places -- or, as he describes it: "Wherever outdoor people have a sense of humor."

Sales of Walker's "Tales From a Game Warden" series have raised more than $40,000 for a scholarship fund at Bethel Baptist Church.

With the mailing of this year's scholarship checks, Walker will have sent more than $20,000 to college students. Even better, he says, he has been able to watch a number of past recipients finish their educations and go on to become active members of the community.

While the "Game Warden" series now includes six books, Walker says he still remembers how it all began.

"It has been really something for a retired Michigan conservation officer who wrote a weekly article called the "Fish Report" to have been able to self-publish a book of those articles titled *A Deer Gets Revenge* and see it grow in sales until it qualified as a self-published best seller."

That debut book is now in its fifth printing, and Walker says there is no sign of sales slowing down.

The other books in the series -- *A Bucket of Bones, From the Land Where the "Big" Fish Live, Humans Are Nuts, Some Call It Luck, Some Skill, But Just Maybe Stupidity (Can We Ever Really Tell?)* and *But! But Honey It Wasn't My Fault* -- are doing equally well.

But the path to success was not necessarily easy, especially since Walker had no idea how to market that first title. Not knowing any better, he just put some books in the trunk of his car and started out to see if he could sell a few.

He stopped at some Upper Peninsula radio stations to ask for their help in spreading the word. He visited local newspapers to see if they would do an article about the books.

The U.P. media did pitch in, as did a newspaper in Green Bay and a staff writer for the *Tuscola County Advisor*, whose subsequent article appeared in a number of newspapers in Michigan's "thumb" and elsewhere.

"Without all these people helping out in the sale of books, the scholarship fund would never have been able to raise all the money it has," Walker says. "And without their help, students could not have received more than $20,000 in scholarships."

Chapter 10

Conservation Officer's Stories
Upper Michigan Tales from a Game Warden's Perspective

So Whose Getting Old?

In our travels through life sometimes things change so fast it is hard to stay up with them. The real problem is that if an old fossil like me brought up some of the changes the younger generation would surely figure we had lost it. Here are a few things to think about.

Some More Ifens

Ifen, you are old enough to wonder what ever happed to the Jewel Tea Man that used to stop by the house each week?

Ifen, you remember that a crank was not Wifee having a bad day, but something you used to start the car with?

Ifen, you remember a metal deer tag, back tags you were supposed to wear, and when red and black checkers were the colors that a real hunter wore during firearm deer season?

Ifen, you remember when turkeys were something that was hunted down south and who ever heard of there being turkeys in Michigan?

Ifen, and you are really showing your age now, you remember when the doctor came by the house when grandpa was sick?

Ifen, you can remember when a **big** logging truck only had one rear axel under it?

Ifen, you figure a three foot piece of garden hose is a Yooper Credit Card.

Ifen, you can remember when logging trucks first came out with a new way to load logs. When some took an old truck transmission and rear end to make a way to load logs with half the work involved?

Ifen, you can remember when snowmobiles first became available to the average Yooper?

This story may put it in perspective. Well this past week sure was an interesting one. Almost a year ago a party got hold of me about speaking at a banquet up at the Best Western in Munising. This weekend get together was for the Antique Snowmobile Club of America. Now this old fossil has trouble remembering things that he is suppose to do next week, let alone writing a note on the margin of last years calendar for this year. But then I never heard another thing about it but kept the weekend open. About a month ago the man called back to make sure I was going to be there. When I got up there I found out why we had never met during the year. The party that had called me was from Southern Illinois and his son was from Alabama!

Now what in the world are people from these areas doing at an antique snowmobile get together? But there were people from all over there. The head of the organization was from Northern Minnesota. But what a fun loving bunch of people they were. You have heard me say for years that the old time snowmobilers were a different group of people all together from those of today and this weekend get together proved it to me once again.

As I walked around looking at some of these old machines it sure brought back memories. In fact, I went through some old pictures I had where my Dad had his old Bolins with a sled hooked to the back with six-eight grandkids going off for a snowmobile ride. Those were the days. If you could get some machines up to 30 miles an hour you thought you were flying and a trip that got you ten-fifteen miles from home could be an all day adventure. But we sure had fun!

As I told them when I spoke there is one thing that really is starting to bother me! If something that came along after you were out of high school and had already done your time in the service is an antique, what does this make Wifee's husband? If something Grandpa Grizz looked at in the showroom, as the newest thing on the market is now an antique, what can I say? But also this old fossil can remember when these now antique sleds were the "New Ones" that the game warden was issued to use on patrol. The

more I looked and the more I thought about it the older I got!
As I said in one of my books when I defined when Dad says to one
of the kids, "You know the other day…." and tells them a story. To
the boy it is a history lesson, but to Dad it seems like it was just
yesterday that he is talking about.

I cannot figure it out, something you threw out behind the barn
when it broke down and was considered a piece of junk is now
really, really valuable and a collectors item, how come as us old
fossils get older they now try to throw us out behind the barn? After
all there are a few still having coffee at Jack's, Hardee's or in
Texas, in the mornings that are twice as old as some of these col-
lectable, antique snowmachines are! So I guess in the eyes of
some collector somewhere we should be getting more valuable
with each passing day.

These people that have held meetings all over the North Country
during the past number of winters were really impressed with the
people at the Best Western and their Yooper hospitality. They even
remarked about how we were able to have a fresh snowfall for
them to enjoy.

Now you have to picture these machines in a "high speed" series
of activities. There were hill climbs, drag races, and oval races,
along with a few other things. But some things have not changed
in all the years these machines have been around. There was one
party that displayed how quick they can stop, when the track
comes off, and jams up under the sled. There were other sleds that
had a distinct weight disadvantage caused by all the years that
have went by since they were new. It had nothing to do with the
sled, but maybe grandma's cooking for the last forty years?

These antique snowmobilers are a great bunch and sure enjoy life.
If you want to see a few of these sleds take a ride over to
Naubinway this weekend where they are having their yearly
antique snowmobile show. Just don't let Charlie tell you any stories
because he is not old enough to be one of us antique's, he just
decided to grow some gray hair and act like one.

I can remember using some of the snowmobiles they are now collecting for antiques on fish patrols out on Saginaw Bay. It sure
makes a person wonder.

Ifen, you remember what a Silver Hawk or a Golden Hawk was? They were the fastest machine a boy could dream of back when I was in high school.

Ifen, you kids think it is a motorcycle you do not need to even shave twice a week yet!

Ifen, you can remember a Studebaker you know what I am talking about.

Ifen, you remember when the local Game Warden drove his own personal car?

Ifen, you remember when a bad day in the office was when you put a piece of carbon paper in backwards?

Ifen, you remember what a piece of carbon paper is?

Ifen, you remember when a Game Warden was mean and green, or at least his uniform was?

Ifen, you remember back in 1952: (Taken from the back of an old county map someone dropped off)

1. Number of Michigan deer hunters: 394,905, Schoolcraft County: 7,216.
2. Number of deer taken: 115,181, Schoolcraft County: 2,816. Obviously these were the legal ones reported. You don't have to report illegal ones.
3. Percent of Successful hunters State: 30.4% Schoolcraft County: 39.0%.
4. Deer killed per square mile: State: 3.01, Schoolcraft County: 2.4.
5. Small Game License issued: State: 627,415, Schoolcraft County: 2,086.
6. Game taken in Schoolcraft County: Rabbits: 262, Grouse: 8,187
7. Fishing License issued: State of Michigan: 1,226,899 1st in nation. Schoolcraft County: 6,225. (And remember back then a wife fished free on her husband's fishing license so she did not have to purchase one.)

Some Suggested Don'ts

Here are some sure ways to improve your chances of getting a ticket from the Game Warden when he comes across you out in the woods. If you really want to make his day just ask him one of the following questions.

1. Are you really a Park Ranger?
2. Do they allow Game Wardens to carry guns?
3. Are you really on a bunny patrol?

Some don'ts when shining:

4. Does your mother know you're out this late?
5. I thought you had to take a physical to be a Game Warden?
6. Or, I thought a Game Warden had to be in good physical condition?
7. Is your attitude always like this or are you just having a bad day?
8. Does your wife really own a doughnut shop?
9. Is this a real ticket?
10. You wouldn't believe this, but this is the third ticket I have gotten for doing this same stupid thing? In fact all the other three were written here at this same spot? But it doesn't bother me because I failed to appear on any of the other three, so this one won't make any difference either?
11. Do Game Wardens get to hunt on duty?
12. Is this how you manage to feed all those kids you have with the items you seize?
13. Does your whole family behave like you do or are you the exception?
14. You mean I really did not have to stop?
15. Why don't you try to catch real criminals for the first time in your career?
16. When did they drop the size and weight requirement for Game Wardens?
17. Do they still have an eyesight requirement for Game Wardens?
18. What's the matter did you get in trouble for missing your quota last month?
19. Are you really on piece-work where you get paid for each ticket you write?

62

20. Are Game Wardens really a sub species of the human race?
21. You know you're the first Game Warden that ever checked me so the law of average is on my side seeing I have been getting away with this for years?
22. Are you sure this law didn't change since I left the house?
23. Was five gallons beyond your mental ability so they dropped it to two and a half?
24. Are you old enough to be out in the woods without a chaper one?
25. Are you one of those environmentalist that never hunted or fished in their life?
26. Do they give Game Wardens bullets for their guns?
27. Do **you** have a snowmobile certificate?
28. You say you're stuck? I'll go get some help.

Chapter 11
Conservation Officer's Stories **Upper Michigan Tales from a Game Warden's Perspective**
Just A Matter Of A Few Dollars

Needless to say there have been a few changes in the way things are done out in the woods. Is it possible that a logger can have umpteen hundred thousand dollars tied up in all their equipment in this day and age? It makes one wonder. Here is an article that was in my stuff in which my Grandpa Theiler was quoted about logging back when dad says, "You know the other day.."

Hot Logging

Well, needless to say a few things have changed in my lifetime. I thought I would let you read a copy of a newspaper article about my Grandpa Harry that I had. Compare this with today's world. This article was from the late 1940's.

Special Correspondent of The Wall Street Journal (William J. Duchaone)

Houghton, Mich.- It's mostly "hot Logging" in Michigan's Upper Peninsula timber country these days.

Demand for lumber, pulpwood, and veneer logs hasn't slacked a bit with the end of the war. Buyers go out in the woods and wait for the logs to fall into their arms under the saws and axes of the lumberjacks. Veneer, paper, and other wood-using companies have expediters on the job to see that the stuff gets loaded and on its way.

Increased use of trucks and portable sawmills also has given extra impetus to hot logging that is, moving the tree to where it's going to be used almost as soon as it's felled.

Howard Blazer, who operates a portable at Redridge, 15 miles from Houghton, and a small woods operation nearby, has cut trees in the morning, run them through his saw and planer before noon, loaded the lumber in the railroad car and had the shipment on its way before nightfall. That's hot logging.

Fifty years ago, when the great white pine forest of this part of the country were being cut into lumber that built the towns and farm-steads of the prairie states, logging was a matter of "cold decking"- stacking up logs in the woods, or on the railroad sidings, for ship-ment in the spring.

Camps Once Frozen In All Winter

In those days the lumberjack went into the woods camp in the fall, stayed all winter, rode the log drive down when the rivers thawed and spent his winter wages on a spree. Then he could make up his mind whether to work in the sawmills during the summer, lie around and pile up a tab at the boardinghouse while he waited for time to go to camp again, or work on a schooner plying to Detroit or Chicago with lumber.

As forest grew thin along the Menominee, the Escanaba, the Ford, the Manistique, and the smaller rivers that spread like the sticks of a fan from Lake Michigan side of Upper Michigan, logging railroads took the rivers place.

Four lumbering companies still operate railroads in the region. They are the Ford Motor Company, at L'Anse, Lake Superior Lumber Corp. at Ontonagon, Bay de Noquet Co. at Nahma, and Cadillac-Soo Lumber Company of Sault Ste. Marie.

The railroads still enjoy a good business on the long hauls. Trainloads of pulpwood move daily to paper mills in Wisconsin's Fox River and Wisconsin River valley's. Also, they move lumber and other forest products from the large mills that still operate in the Upper Peninsula.

Trucks, though, are much used for both short and long hauls. Drive any day on Upper Michigan's highways, and you see truckload after truckload of logs rolling to the mills. Birch and maple veneer logs travel 200 miles from the Copper Country to the Birds Eye Veneer mills at Houghton. Other logs move south into Wisconsin.

One reason there's so much paper, excelsior, veneer and box-making timber left is that the old white pine logger scorned hemlock, spruce, balsam, and other conifer species, as well as hard-woods, as "weeds." That's why employment in the Upper Peninsula forest today. At 30,000 persons, is almost as high as it was in the white pine loggers hayday.

Truck Operators Make Quick Profits

Truck drivers are paid 80 cents an hour, and usually get in consid-erable overtime each week. So, they make good money. Some buy trucks and log trailers, as soon as they save enough to make a down payment, to haul on contract. A good outfit cost from $1,800 to $2,000, but some operators have got their investment back the first year.

A truck owner-driver pays for the gasoline, oil and repairs on his equipment, and usually figures he should make $15 to $20 a day for himself. Harry Theiler of Tomahawk, Wis, who operates Theiler Brother woods camps on the Salmon Trout creek, 15 miles south-west of Houghton, pays the truckers $6 per 1,000 board feet on a four mile log haul from the woods to the Copper Range railroad siding.

Logging trucks undergo heavy wear and tear. The hauler has to get a new one every four or five years. Tractors are replacing horses for skidding logs in the woods, although some timber jobbers retain a few teams for use when they want to snake logs out for short dis-tances. Under some conditions, it is more economical to use hors-es.

Another stimulus for hot logging in recent years has been the advent of the bulldozer, which has greatly simplified and cheap-ened road making in the woods. A bulldozer, powered with a heavy Diesel motor, is an expensive piece of equipment, selling for about $8,000, but loggers regard it as essential.

"I couldn't get along without my bulldozer," said Harry Theiler, who was a road building contractor before he re-entered the logging business in war-time. "It does the work of 200 men."

Bulldozer Makes Roads in Hurry

Theiler's bulldozer, equipped with a LeTourheau blade, cuts a swath through the hardwood forest at the rate of three-fourths to one mile a day, uprooting huge trees and pushing them off the right of way, scraping and filling here and there to make a smooth surface truck road. Theiler estimates his road building cost less than $90 per mile. The dozer operator is the top of the wage earners; he gets one dollar per hour.

While some of Upper Michigan's large sawmills have gone out of business in recent years because of the exhaustion of their timber supply, the portable sawmills has increased in number, particularly after Pearl Harbor. Someone has nicknamed them "popgun mills" in this country. In the Ozarks and other parts of the South they are called pecker wood, ground-rattler and coffeepot mills.

One advantage of the portable mill is that it can be located in the midst of a small, isolated timber tract, thereby eliminating long hauling costs. These "popguns" represent a wide range of cost and productive capacity. Some use an old automobile engine for motive power. The better ones operated by Diesel motors or electricity. Cost of setting one up will vary from $1500 to $1,500. Such a mill produces all the way from 2,000 to 12,000 board feet a day.

Although most Peninsula lumber is still cut by the big mills, the portables were an important factor in manufacturing much-needed lumber and railroad cross-ties during the war. Because good prices are paid for lumber regardless of grade, some "popgun" operators are making good money. Yearly incomes of $10,000 to $20,000 have been reported.

A portable mill, producing about 10,000 board feet a day, can get along with a crew of eight to 10 men. In some instances, they are producing more lumber per worker than the large sawmills employing 100 to 150 men.

Portable mill operators, of course, are living in lush times. Selling is no problem. They pay no attention to letters from prospective buyers, for they have orders on hand for every stick they can produce. Their lumber is shipped out green. There is no need to kiln-dry or season it to sell it nowadays.

Fancy prices, all at ceiling, are being paid for logs, lumber, and pulpwood. One man recently cut down two white-pine trees which scaled 4,950 board feet. Sawed into lumber they brought him $550. First and second grade birch lumber bring $131 a thousand feet, and the lowly hemlock sells at $45.

Timber jobbers get equally attractive prices for their logs. No.1 maple commands $84. At one time before the war, the prices were as low as $38 and $30. The ceiling price on hemlock logs was raised last November 29th from $24 to $28.

68

Picture of Marv with one of his pups

Marv out in the woods with one of his dogs

Chapter 12
Conservation Officer's Stories **Upper Michigan Tales from a Game Warden's** **Perspective**
They Hate It When You Do That

I guess if you have been at any job long enough you run into times when you have to go to alternate plan B in order to get the results you want. The only problem is that in law enforcement for some reason when they realize what happened they tend to think they got snookered. Here are a few of those cases where we started out with nothing, but took what we had and ran with it.

Sturgeon From The Manistique River

When you work as a Game Warden there are always those stories you hear about someone taking something illegally, but you are never in the right place at the right time to do anything about it.

If you are at all familiar with Manistique, where I worked, you know that the Manistique River runs right through town into Lake Michigan. There is also a dam right in town and a flume that runs along the river to carry water to the paper mill. In the spring of the year when the water gets high from the winter snows melting and spring rains they open the dam to let the water flow faster into Lake Michigan.

A lot of times when they lower the water in the flumes by allowing it to run through the river channel there are fish in the flume that came up out of Lake Michigan to spawn. I always heard that there was Lake Sturgeon left high and dry when this happened. Of course the Game Warden always heard about those that were taken after the fact.

On this morning just as I was starting out on patrol I stopped at a local business for coffee. While I was there a party came up to me and told me about two people that had come into a gas station the night before to show them the two sturgeon they had taken out of the river. They were in the trunk of their car. There was no doubt in my mind that what I was told was true, but I had less than nothing to go on.

I poked around until I found out what type vehicle the two people were in that had the sturgeon. I pin pointed the time they had them and checked to see just when the dam had been opened and the water routed into the river. I got all kinds of information, but still nothing in which I could use.

My next step was to do some research on Sturgeon and I found out a number of things that did not help matters either. I found that Sturgeon are one of the few fish that do not have any scales, but have more of a prehistoric hide on them. So out the window went my fish theory of hopefully finding something in their trunk that would prove they had transported some Sturgeon in it. I ask if there was anything else that could have come off the fish to prove they were in the trunk and was told it was really unlikely.

So I kept digging around until I had all the evidence I could collect about the time, the place, all the people they had shown the Sturgeon too, and everything else I could find out about. When I had all this I figured I might as well throw one of those "Holy Mary" passes down field and see what happens.

So we picked up the subjects and decided to talk to them. We read them their rights and told them why we wanted to talk to them. They were asked if they wanted to talk to us and they agreed. So we told them that we knew they had taken a couple of Sturgeons, when they took them, where they had taken them from, and that they had them in the trunk of their car at such a time and place.

The key to this whole thing was to make them believe we had a whole lot more information and evidence than we really did. We did not lie to them, but neither did we tell them what we didn't have. It ends up being kind of like a fill-in-the-blank quiz you took when you were in school. You tell them with an attitude of letting them think you know more than you really do and let them fill in the blanks. The amazing thing is that most of the times if things go right they do.

When you have everything rolling along just right you suggest they write out the story of what really happened that night so we will have all the facts in order. Believe it or not more times than not they will take the piece of paper you give them and write out just what took place and how they had violated the law.

When everything is done and they sign it you have a written confession of everything that took place. I have never had any problems with the person that was involved, but more than once a family member would get involved thinking we really took advantage of the person.

The funny thing is, to this person, it did not matter that they really had taken something illegally; they felt it was wrong to get them to give us a written confession about what they had done.

A Real Case Of Discrimination

Living up here *In The Land Where BIG Fish Live* one gets to see some real nice fish. One week there was a picture of a BIG fish in the local newspaper that really got me thinking. It has to be a classic case of discrimination if there ever was one.

A fishermen can catch a nice pike or musky, anything more than twenty pounds, and right away runs down to get it mounted so he can show it off for the next fifty years to anyone that will listen to his story. Let a brooktrout fisherman catch a nice 3-4 pound brookie and off he goes to the local taxidermist. It could be a twenty some inch walleye or even a real nice perch and our fisherman is willing to pay big bucks so he can forever brag about his big catch. This is just a way of life for any fisherman.

But! Let a guy spear or catch a hundred to two hundred pound sturgeon and what do they do? Does it ever cross their mind to get this two hundred pound fish mounted? (In all my travels as a Game Warden I cannot recall ever seeing a mounted sturgeon anywhere.)

You ask why? Could it be because they are flat **ugly**! Could you just see our happy fisherman coming home with a hundred and fifty pound sturgeon that goes from one side of the tailgate of his pickup to the other, so he calls his wife out to see what he had caught as he beams from ear to ear.

She stands there looking at this bionically ugly fish laying there and hears her hubby say, "Honey, I'm thinking of having this trophy mounted to place over the fireplace mantel in the living room." Something may get hung on the wall all right, but it won't be the fish, just maybe the fisherman?

I really have to wonder in the world that fish live in how the "rights" of Sturgeon are upheld? How would you like to look like something out of the stone age, swim along the bottom of the lake with a mouth like a big vacuum cleaner, sucking up all the junk from the lake bottom and blowing it out the vents on the side of your head?

All the other fish are swimming around poking fun at the way you look and the way you swim. They say mean things about what your mother looks like. They even go as far as to sometimes question if you are really a fish at all.

In fact you have to grow up wondering if even a mother Sturgeon can look at one of her offspring and brag about how cute he really is. Unless of course she would cover things by saying, "Jr. sure looks like his daddy." **UGLY!**

So if you ever feel left out and maybe think you were discriminated against just be glad you are not a Sturgeon.

There Had To Be Some Kind Of Punishment

In some cases that a Game Warden runs into there is really no punishment for the crime that has already been committed. If some person under the age of sixteen goes out and shoots a deer or took a couple of fish out of season there was not much you could really do about it.

Back in the Stone Age when I started out you could scare the fire out of them in Probate Court with a judge that told them he had better never see them again. But as the new generation of Probate Judges took over it seemed that these underage violators had more rights than even the adult violators did. So it was usually not worth the time it took to take one of them to probate court.

This being the case you at times had to adlib to make justice work.

On this particular evening it was just getting dark when I went to work. It was the spring of the year and I was going to work some of the ditches where I knew a lot of pike came up to spawn.

First let me say that one of the biggest jokes in our justice system is the fact that youth can get a drivers license at sixteen, but not have to pay the penalty for their actions until they reach their seventeenth birthday. For a lot of youth this means a year to go out and raise cain before judgment day ever comes.

As dark approached I was going down a gravel road without any lights on when I saw the glow from a lantern way across a field in a draining ditch. I parked my car and started off across the field heading towards the light. As I walked and walked I soon realized that I had misjudged where the light was. It soon became apparent that they were a whole lot closer to the next road than the one where I had parked the patrol car. But I kept on trucking.

I finally came up to the area where the light was down in the creek and could tell there were three people looking for fish. I tried to slide down the bank to get close to them in order to try and grab them before they could run. They had a sack with them that I figured had some fish in it the way they were carrying it.

I tried to come up behind them without being seen when one of them must have heard me because all of a sudden they tossed their spears and sack and took off running up the bank on the far side of the creek. I was working by myself and seeing I was across the creek there was no way I was ever going to get across and even come close to catching them.

Maybe I was watching too much TV at the time and they must have been watching too much also, because I yelled, "Hold it right there or I'll shoot! Come on back here!" All three of them stopped dead in their tracks and walked back down the hill to where I was standing.

I soon saw why, here came three youth about 14-15 years of age. All this work, coming across almost a mile of wooded field in the dark only to find out I did not even have any keepers! What now?

I took their spears and the sack with the fish in it and walked out to the road that was nearest to where I had caught them. We dumped the fish out on the ground and they had speared five real nice pike. There was no way I was going to waste my time taking them to probate court where nothing would happen so I thought up the next best thing.

I reached under my coat and took out a good knife I carried and handed it to them. I then asked them if they knew where an older couple lived down the road a ways figuring they did seeing we all lived within a few miles of where I had caught them.

When they told me they did, I told them they had a project while I walked back to get my patrol car. They were told that by the time I returned with my car they had better have all the pike filleted out and we were going down the road so they could give them to this older man that I knew could not get out fishing anymore.

By the time I got back they had them all done so we placed them in a plastic bag I had and drove down to give them to this older couple. I really think this guy knew all the time what had happened because he grew up where he now lived and needless to say the creek had been there all his life. Even when he was the age of these three boys that had brought him a present of out of season pike.

Chapter 13
Conservation Officer's Stories **Upper Michigan Tales from a Game Warden's Perspective**
The Old School

Maybe every age thinks the same thing I don't really know, but for some reason I always figured I hit the tail end of the best times. This was before someone invented computers, cell phones, pagers, and all these other gadgets that were suppose to make life a whole lot easier. Who were they trying to kid? Here are a few things that will let you better understand how much things have changed and yet stayed the same.

It Was Just The Way It Was

If I hear this remark once a day during hunting season I hear it a dozen times, "We never see a Conservation Officer anymore." There can be any number of reasons for this, but let me give you a few ways things have changed.

Back when I first started working as a Conservation Officer would you believe that a good number of the officers never even carried a pistol when they went to work. In fact you were not issued a belt like the one that now carries your holster, clips for your pistol, handcuffs, and other gear until a number of years later.

Even after they were issued there were still those old timers that could not get used to having to regularly wear a pistol as a standard part of their uniform.

In fact I can remember going to pistol shoots, back then we had the old 38 caliber Colts, where some of the older officers had to clean their pistol in order to get it to work. A lot of them just never felt a need to always carry a sidearm unless you felt you were doing something where it was needed.

Believe it or not back in those days we had two uniforms, one for winter and then a summer one. In the winter you had a green shirt as your uniform shirt, but in the summer time you had a short sleeve tan colored shirt for a uniform shirt. Of course most all these shirts were made of wool like you would never find in this day and age. I don't think an officer could wear one out in the thirty years he worked. Needless to say you may outgrow them, but you would never wear this material out.

The uniforms you were issued came with a set of strict rules for just how they were to be worn. You have to remember back then a good number of the officers were former military men that saw only one way to wear a uniform and that was with respect and pride. If you didn't want to do this you could just take it off and hit the road.

I can remember when I received my first uniform that we were issued a couple of pair of Wolverine boots. When they were given to us they were brown colored, but they had a white sole on them. The tailor that issued these boots to us new officer gave each of us a jar of black tanning paint and we were flat told that the white better never show up on these boots after today.

It sure was a different world back then, but you would have had to be there to feel the camaraderie that the officers had for each other. A lot of great memories still live in my mind about those old timers.

Some Stories I Never Understood

I don't know where this story came from and the things that cause the story to be retold and laughed about by those old timers never seemed to wear out for them.

Where this story got started and what happened I never knew, but it seems that there was someone that tried and even made it into the old Conservation Department as a Conservation Officer years ago. For some reason this party did not make the grade and he was let go from the department.

I don't know how many times years later I would be going somewhere with a car load of these older officers and they would get talking about this guy when we went by a restaurant that was part of a chain. Each time we did one of the older officers would remark, "We (The Department) sure taught him a lesson didn't we!" and they would all start laughing like crazy.

It seems that this party that had tried out to be a Conservation Officer and was released from the department had went out and managed to become a millionaire.

Now you have to remember that back then a Game Warden was not making a whole lot of money and if he were to lose his job he would probably get a raise on welfare. So whenever these officers saw a sign that reminded them of the guy that couldn't cut the mustard they had to either laugh or cry when reminded of it.

We Were A Family, Remember That

This is an article I wrote about a widow of an officer killed in the line of duty when I heard how the state had treated her. A retired Conservation Officer worked for years trying to help a fellow officers wife after her husband was killed in the line of duty and she got the short end of the stick on his retirement. I would hate to say how many trips he made to Lansing and back trying to get her what she deserved. The last time I talked to him it looked like she would get it.

I would like to tell you about a horror story that was once again brought to my attention. During the week Wifee and I were at Hardee's for coffee when a retired Conservation Officer I knew came in. Seeing I was outnumbered at coffee three to one (Three women against one guy) I decided to go over and talk to him.

He told me he was once again on his way to Lansing to fight a battle for a widow lady that has been trying for almost thirty years to get what she rightly deserves.

Almost thirty years ago this lady watched her husband get ready and go off to work one evening during bear season. As he left home on that evening to work with another game warden there was no way in her thoughts that this would be the last time she would ever say good-by to her husband. I guess all those that are married to people that work law enforcement are aware that something could happen, but really never expect it to.

On this evening these two game wardens decided to check one of the local dumps where they knew there were a number of bear that came in to feed. As they checked out the dump they came across a pickup that they felt should be checked out. As this officer walked up to check out the pickup it took off hitting him and dragging him to his death.

After thirty years of working as a Michigan Conservation Officer this officer had left home for the last time leaving his wife and family never to return. But, believe it or not this is not the only tragic thing that resulted from what took place on that evening in a dump here in the U.P. Not only did this lady lose her husband, she also for some reason lost her right to the income that she should have received from her husband losing his life doing his job as a game warden for the citizens of the state of Michigan. Here is what I was told before and once again told about in Hardee's this week.

It seems that this widow of a Conservation Officer killed in the line of duty was never informed of his rightful benefits and never told the options she had as a result of his death. Some records show he had over thirty years of service with the state of Michigan. But the state says he had only twenty-nine years, eleven month of service. Which really should not make any difference in this case. But on account of this the widow was told she had only a real, real small amount of money coming even though her husband had been killed in the line of duty.

Now almost thirty years later the fight is still going on. The lady now in her eighties has for years been raising chickens and selling eggs just to try to keep her head above water since the death of her husband.

But still this tragic and unjust story continues to go on. It seems when this story was brought before the legislator members of both parties wondered how this could have ever happened in a state like ours. So a bill was introduced to correct this injustice and passed by members of both parties to correct this wrong and give this widow justice after almost thirty years of injustice. There was just no way that anyone could think about not supporting something like this, after all she had lost her husband in uniform working for the people of this great state. How could anyone as a citizen of Michigan not do right and help out an eighty-three year old lady having to sell eggs just to get something to eat after the price that this family had paid serving us?

Or should I say almost everybody agreed there was just no way those representing, you and I, the citizens of this state, would not want to correct this tragic mistake from thirty years ago. What I was told was one person that did not feel that things should be corrected even after both parties of the legislator approved doing it. There was this man that is collecting around $70,000.00 a year for his retirement from the state legislator, after having received a kicker of $23,000.00 when he retired. Or should I say while he is still working, but collecting a retirement from the state of Michigan. When he gets done with this job I am told he will receive seventy to ninety percent of his pay in another retirement from the people of the state of Michigan. This total should be well more than $100,000.00 from the citizens of the state of Michigan when everything is said and done. This man who will receive all this vetoed the bill that would have corrected this injustice to a lady who had said good-by to her husband one evening and gave him up to the citizens of Michigan.

I ask you why do things like this happen in this day and age? Why does a wife that sacrificed this much have to live like this after the price that was paid by this family? So every time you sit down to have a breakfast with a couple of eggs think about the little, eighty-three year old widow lady that has to sell eggs just to make ends meet after all she gave to those that love and use the great outdoors of our state.

Something New!

I have had so many people ask about the license plate that has been on my vehicles for more than twenty-five years I thought I would have some made up. These license plates let people know about one of the best tools to help you raise your kids. Please let people at work & sportsmen's groups know about it & where they can order one.

Theses license plates sell for $5.00 please add $2.00 for shipping and handling. There is a better rate for volume orders. You can order them from: J.A.W.'S Publications, 530 Alger Ave. Manistique, MI 49854 Phone: 906-341-2082

The License plate is made from Polytuff material and is a blue background with yellow writing. It really looks Sharp.

Chapter 14
Conservation Officer's Stories **Upper Michigan Tales from a Game Warden's Perspective**
Hung Up On The Job

There are always some stories that never get old because if they were told by the modern Game Wardens you would know they could never happen the way they did because of the way their equipment is made today. Needless to say the following story could never happen with the bumpers there are on today's vehicles.

Hung Up On The Job

In the area called The River Road there were a number of clans that had their own way of thinking about how life ought to operate. In fact "according to rumor" there were those back in the hayday of deer hunting that used to collect nice bucks the week before the firearm deer season and then go around and sell them to the Trolls that came up to the area deer hunting.

Of course you know that nobody would really do a thing like this, don't you? But then again I could give you a few names that were given to me about some of those that made their "Christmas Bonus" during the deer season selling nice bucks.

On this night the Game Warden was working the area of River Road that turns down over the hill to go along the river to Germfask. Needless to say after you dropped over the hill from an area that was called Curran's Orchard and the fields in the area with the apple trees you were going beyond civilization. Most of the locals felt it was an area where Game Wardens feared to operate.

The officer that was working was running without lights when he spotted a vehicle running slow along the road and watched them use a light to try and find a deer. In most cases if it was for their own use it did not matter if it had horns or not. As the old saying goes, "You don't eat the horns anyway!"

The Game Warden pulled up behind the shiners vehicle and

turned on his lights and off they went. Just before you hit the open fields where there is more than one way to go, there are two real sharp right angle curves. The poachers figured that in the area where these curves were, seeing they had to slow down anyway, they would pull a "slicky" on the warden.

So right after they rounded the second curve where the road straightened out again, and usually they would just floor it and take off, they slammed on their brakes and stopped right in the middle of the road hoping the warden's car would run into them. It worked perfect, just as planned!

They then floored their car to take off figuring to leave the shocked Game Warden in their dust. Peddle to the floor, engine roaring, and wheels spinning, off they failed to go!

It seems with some of those old cars, as we all remember that are old enough, they had a real bumper back then that had a bad habit when vehicles came together just right. Here go our poachers trying to make a run for home with just a slight problem. It was soon apparent that the front bumper on the warden's car had jumped over the back bumper on the poacher's car and the two vehicles were hooked together.

There can be no worse feeling than spotting the Game Warden in your back window and knowing the reason he is there and not about to leave is your own fault.

You Have Until The End Of The Week!

Years ago, long before I was around, Game Wardens were appointed by the county and usually worked right in the area where they were appointed. On a lot of occasions this made for some rather interesting situations. In fact even after they became State Conservation Officers for years they were more or less picked to work an area where they knew all about what was going on. We have all heard the saying, "Sometimes the best Game Warden was the best violator because he knew all the tricks they used."

In this case, and I heard it from a relative, there was this party from Manistique that just got word that he was going to become a Game

Warden. He was related to one of the largest clans in the area and he would be working part of the area that would include the River Road area.

Back then you have to remember that beaver trapping was for big bucks in this time and age. As I have stated before there were times you got more than a dollar an inch for a nice, large beaver blanket. So if this be the case, there were sure to be a few of those that figured that seasons interfered with their rights to make an income and feed their families. So it was not uncommon if the pelts were prime to trap after the close of season and maybe even get a head start on the season if conditions were right.

Also remember that back then you could not purchase a beaver-trapping license after the opening of season. So it probably made good business sense to know how many licenses you needed before you went to the Game Warden's house to purchase them. Because back in those days you purchased trapping licenses direct from the local warden.

So if the limit for a single license was ten beaver and you already had twenty-six out in the barn and you figured in a good season you could easily catch twenty more you would need five licenses. Well, maybe you had better get six just in case. So you would purchase a trapping license for yourself, the wife, the two boys, the girl, and the family dog to cover all the beaver you would need to seal at the end of season.

This after season beaver sealing also was done by the local warden.

So here a local native, had changed to the other side of the fence, but this did not mean that he did not know who some of the local trappers were that had extended the season on both ends. So he figured he had to be fair so he went around, so I was told, and informed all the family members that there was going to be a new warden in town and they had until the end of the week to square things away and get rid of any illegal hides they may have around.

Right or wrong he figured this was the only fair way to handle things, but for years I did hear some interesting stories about this officer and the last I heard most of them came from the McMillan

Honest Officer

In the years when I started working as a Game Warden it was almost normal for an officer to work until he hit the big 70 and then he had to retire. It is funny how things have changed over the years, but back then it was just the way things were done.

Needless to say when you had those officers my age, in their early twenties, working with those officers pushing seventy there were some interesting times.

I can recall one officer that worked in the county next to mine, that I was always told patrolled the 19th hole at the local golf club most of the time. When he did decide to work needless to say I would be the one that would have to work with him.

Needless to say I was soon to learn that when you got up to pushing seventy you went to a different system of law enforcement. We would go out to work shiners in the early evening and sit near a cornfield until we saw someone using a spotlight to try and see deer out in the field.

We would sneak up behind the vehicle shining and turn on the blue light to pull them over. After they pulled over and stopped this older officer would say, "Pull up along side of them." He would then roll down his window and ask the driver, "You guys don't have any firearms in the vehicle with you, do you?"

When he received his answer, which was always in the negative, he would thank them and off we would go.

In all the times we stopped someone who was shining never once did one of them say, "Ya, I have my rifle, loaded and uncased sitting on the front floor in case we should see a deer."

The only thing I could figure was that this older officer had all the shiners in his neck of the woods cleaned up. But if this was the case I could never figure out why there were so many of them shining while having a rifle with them over in my county that was just a few miles away?

Chapter 15
Conservation Officer's Stories **Upper Michigan Tales from a Game Warden's Perspective**
How An Old Game Warden Became An Exspurt

This will give you a better idea of how the old Game Warden became an Exspurt on whatever they did back in the Good Old Days.

First off you have to understand that in today's world an employer goes out and purchases an Exspurt. But as we all know years ago you hired an employee with the good habits, character, and work ethics and you spent time training them to perform the job they were hired to do.

Here are a couple of examples that I was involved with and needless to say life was different back then.

You'll Get A Bang Out Of This

Needless to say when you were hired back when I was looking for a job you never knew just what you were getting into. Back then a person was expected to do whatever the job required and there were not Exspurts to perform every little task. I will admit that there were those that were hired as a specialist in some areas. In this case there were those Game Wardens that were called state trappers.

On this day I received a call from one of these state trappers telling me there had been a complaint of beaver problems on some of the drainage ditches in the southwest part of the county.

Now you have to understand that Tuscola County where I was working at the time was basically flat from north to south and east to west. There were about two hills in the whole county that would not really be classified as hills in most counties. Within this county farming is big, so the whole county water table is controlled by a massive series of drainage ditches. In a county like this the county drain commissioner is right up there with the apostles as far as power goes. If he should call and complain that beaver are causing a problem, and beaver are controlled by the state, guess who gets the call.

The state trapper and I went out and looked over the area where the beaver dam was. If you were to class beaver dams ranging on a 1 to 10 scale this was at least a 9 and could have even been a perfect 10. The dam itself was well over ten feet high all the way across a main drainage ditch.

The trapper looked at me and asks, "Have you ever used dynamite to blow a beaver dam before?" Now needless to say I had come across a few cherry bombs and a M-80 or two, but this was a little out of my class.

We went into the ditch below the dam and took some long poles and worked them into the face of the dam making a hole about five-six inches in diameter under the dam itself. A beaver dam being made of mud and sticks it takes a while to work into the dam far enough to have an effect when the explosives are placed into it.

There were at least a half a dozen holes made into the dam and these were packed with the dynamite that had a blasting cap placed in it. After this was done we ran telephone line back far enough over the rim of the ditch back into a field where we would be safe when the charge was set off. Here we took a little break and got ready to see what success our project would have.

Now understand I am the flunky here and the state trapper is the Exspurt in the removal of beaver dams. Of course I might add that he was an Exspurt in his field up north where beaver are suppose to live out in the great north woods. So this drainage ditch beaver problem was new to both of us, a fact I did not realize at the time.

The trapper said to me, "I don't know what we will accomplish because this beaver dam is so thick and tall the charge may not do much to it." I'm thinking, OK, you're the Exspurt.

So he touches off the dynamite and all that appeared to happen was the dam jumped up in the air a couple of feet and then settled back down into the drainage ditch. As things cleared up you could see a couple of small streams of water coming through the middle of the dam, but that was all.

All of a sudden there was a load "whooosh" and our beaver dam was going down the drainage ditch on the front of a wall of water that was unreal!

Here I was to find out, after looking at his shocked face and listening to him talk in a daze, "I never realized all the water that was backed up by that dam!"

Neither one of us realized that in the area where all these ditches are the water a lot of times does not spread out over the area around the dam, but just keeps backing up in the ditches. So needless to say our project was too successful.

So here goes this six-seven foot wall of water rushing down through this drainage ditch towards a river where it connects down stream. There is one slight problem that came with this, the drainage ditch connected with the river right north of a little town that the river passed through.

We later heard that the people at the local fair in this little town got an extra surprise when the river all of a sudden reached its banks right next to the fairground with trees, mud and all the refuge from a blown beaver dam, but thank goodness, never came over the banks. If from what I heard it sure had people wondering for a minute.

For quite a while I heard talk around the county in my travels from people wondering what caused the river to act like this on a nice, calm, sunny day and there was no way I was going to confess what I knew to them.

How We Learned

In the course of my travels as a Game Warden I had heard horror stories about some of the things that had taken place when officers were sent out to blow beaver dams. It is totally amazing what can happen when you send a couple of Exspurts out with a trunk load of explosives and tell them to remove a beaver dam.

I heard stories of train bridges being knocked out of commission, county roads where the culverts were reshaped, times when everything was removed, but the beaver dam. But still whenever someone had a problem with beaver they called on the Exspurts to come and take care of it.

So here I was working a new area and one of the first things I had was a complaint through the District Office about a beaver problem. Am I lucky or what? Here as in the other case the beaver had blocked a creek where it was flatland all around it. Only in this case the creek was not very deep so the water just backed up all over the countryside. When it started to flood some of the county roads the Exspurts were once again called in.

Now I had never been in charge of blowing a beaver dam before, but I guess seeing I had been on the job for a few years by now and had had coffee with a state trapper or two this now qualified me as an Exspurt.

When I explained to the boss that I had never blown a beaver dam or even used explosives on my own before he said, "No problem I'll send someone along to help you."

Now you have to read between the lines here, he did not say he would send someone along that knew how to use explosives, he only said he would send along a helper. When I heard who the helper was, who had used explosives before, I was not greatly relieved. This guy was one of those that could have an accident putting on his shoes in the morning. In fact, if there had been an award given for the Game Warden for the most accident reports in their career this guy would have surely been in first place.

In fact, it flashed through my mind that just a few days before, I had went by his house and found him with the whole taillight assembly for his patrol vehicle sitting on the kitchen table in at least nine zillion pieces. (This was one of those taillight units that went all the way across some of the older patrol cars.) Here sat my explosive Exspurt with a half dozen tubes of super glue trying to put this puzzle back together because he didn't want to have to do another accident report. But off we went.

Things had improved with what we were using to blow beaver

dams from the early part of my career. Now we had what was called kinetics explosives. What we used looked like Tupperware glasses, with a top, filled with a white powder. You would then take a tube of pink liquid and pour it onto the white powder and let it soak in. Each of these tubes when ready to use were equivalent to a stick and a half of dynamite. You would then tape a blasting cap to the side of the tub and you were ready to use it.

Of course all this was explained to me by the accident prone Exspurt that was sent along to help me. In fact, for some reason it did not set my mind at ease when he started to explain that the tubes of explosives by themselves were harmless, you could do about anything you wanted to them and they would not explode.

But! Then he explained that the danger was with the blasting caps. He explained that we must make sure the wires were connected because even the static electricity in the air could set them off. Great!

So here we are knee deep in mud where you couldn't take off running if you wanted too, but then again it wouldn't do any good, taping a blasting cap to the side of a tube with explosives in it that would make parts of you an astronaut if it went off. Then you had to take the wires from the blasting cap apart and hook them to the telephone wire that you ran far enough away to get you clear of the explosion.

I was informed by the Exspurt that if you got the blasting cap wires separated and hooked to the telephone wire without it going off you were in the clear because the other end of the telephone wires were hooked together. Of course if it didn't work you really would not have to worry about it either.

In some cases you would have a series of charges across the face of a big dam so it was a nerve-racking job getting them all wired together.

We finally got them all hooked up and walked to the far end of the wire to set the charge off. Of course back in those days some people had to take a break for a cigarette after all this work so we were standing there talking while he finished his smoke.

We used a D-cell flashlight battery to set off the blasting cap, this is how touchy they were, it took almost nothing to set them off. As we were talking I was getting a flashlight battery out of one of those Maglites that we all had when all of a sudden there was a big "whoosh" and the whole swamp went up in the air to the treetops! Mud, rocks, stumps, and everything the dam was made of. It seems like when the wires hit the side of my flashlight there was enough juice in it to set off the blasting caps.

On top of this we may have just under estimated the strengths of this beaver dam, because I'm not sure we not only removed the beaver dam but may have created a small inland lake where it once stood. At least the hole in the ground was big enough.

But I survived another blasting trip with an Exspurt and to tell the truth this was the last one I got sent out on and I have to confess I do not miss going on these projects Exspurt or not.

Life Changes

Well, every once in a while I guess we all have flashbacks to things that make us sit and laugh when we think about them years later. If it wasn't so funny after some of the changes I have seen I would sit and cry about what we have lost.

With the way the bugs are at times in early summer and the great crop of mosquitoes that we have it brings back some memories of yesteryear.

Back in the "Good Old Days" it was usually after a wet spring like we have had, plus the melting of the winter snows, that we would receive some beaver complaints from people living in the area where I worked. In both cases the people in the counties I was assigned to would not know a real hill if they saw one. Both were as flat as can be, so whenever beaver dammed up a stream the water would back up forever. When this happened back then they called the Game Warden.

On this particular day we received a complaint up in the area off Stutts Creek Road. The dam was a good sized dam and there was brush all around the area where the dam was built. It was a hot, muggy day, with no wind at all, and the humidity had to be about as high as it can reach. You could sweat to death just leaning against a tree.

I had one of these "new era" officers with me that they had found somewhere down in the asphalt jungle near Detroit. We walked into the area of the beaver dam and had to spend some time tearing out the dam so the water would work its way through it. You do this in enough spots and the water pressure will sometimes take the dam out.

On this day you had to do this without breathing to hard. It was hot, sweaty work where the bugs were so thick you could not take a deep breath or you would swallow at least a million-zillion-billion of them in one gulp. If the mosquitoes did not swarm and remove all the blood from your body before you could defend yourself, the black flies would come in and remove a hunk of you to take over to sit on a stump and chew on. When these two were not feasting on you, the deer flies would come in for lunch.

Whenever you were on a project like this it became mind over matter! If you were out of your mind, the bugs would no longer matter. We finally got the job done and called it a day.

A couple of weeks later I received a call from the bosses in the Big House telling me I had to meet them at Higgins Lake. It appeared that this "new era" conservation officer had turned me into Lansing for taking her on that beaver dam complaint and humiliating her with all the bugs that were there. What? They had to be kidding me, but they weren't.

I went down to meet with them and after they told me what the complaint was I looked at them like they had been on the brain-sucking machine in the Big House too long. Now both of these people had come through the ranks as a Game Warden in the U.P., so why was I even here?

They ask me what I had to say? So I asked both of them, "Have you ever been on a beaver complaint on a hot, muggy day in the U.P.?" "Yes", "Did you ever run into a time when the bugs were so bad you would swallow a dozen every time you took a deep breath?" "Yes", "Did you have any control over all the bugs?" "NO",

"Did you not just grit it out and do what had to be done and figure it went with the job as a conservation officer? "Yes", I had stated my case.

What more could they say, but cases like this were the beginning of the end for Game Wardens, as we knew them for all the years they had been around. When they can file a grievance against the black flies and mosquitoes in the U.P. and someone in the Big House is willing to listen what's the only way to solve the problem? You're right and you wonder why in some areas you hear, "I never see a conservation officer anymore." Have you checked for bugs?

So if you hope to get away with anything, go back into the deepest swamp with the most mosquitoes, black flies, and deer flies you can find and go for it! You only better hope you don't do it in the area where you have one of those dinosaurs from the old school working, because he just might come walking back in there to check you out.

Of course if you are one of those that plays the percentage game you might be all set. I will have to admit that with each passing retirement things are surely on your side. But then again is it worth it?

Chapter 16
Conservation Officer's Stories **Upper Michigan Tales from a Game Warden's** **Perspective**
Wifee And The Kids

I think one of the more interesting things about working, as a Game Warden in the great outdoors was the fact that it was a family affair back in those days. Needless to say times have changed, but back in the "Good Old Days" the whole family liked to think they were junior game wardens.

Please! Don't Tell Me That!

Please don't tell Wifee about this because being a mother she might not understand.

I forget just what was taking place at church on this evening, but I do remember that I was left at home with my two young boys. Now when dad is left in charge it is really hard to tell what might take place.

We had been horse playing around the house, the three of us, when I received a call from the sheriff's department about someone shining on a road just a few miles from the house.

In the area where I was working at the time there were not state police personal that worked the area on a regular basis. The sheriff department stated that all their cars were tied up at the time and they had nobody to send on the complaint.

I figured where there is a will, there is a way, so I told the boys we were going out to check on some poachers. Both boys were already in their PJ's, so I placed them in their sleeping bags and took them out and placed them on the floor in the back seat of my car. Off we went to see what was going on.

We went down the highway to hit the gravel road where the shining complaint had come from. When I turned down this road I spotted a vehicle shining a field about a half mile down the road from where I was.

I came up behind this vehicle and told my boys to stay down on the floor when I got out to see if the shiners were legal or not.

I walked up to the vehicle that was shining and talked to the people in it and checked them out and found out they were legal. So I returned home with my two junior game wardens and swore them to secrecy about our nighttime adventure. It was years later when it finally came out just what we had done.

I Hate It When You Tell Me That!

It never seemed to fail whenever I went out to work and had one of those days when nothing went right I would return home to this.

Here would be the kids running up to meet me at the door to inform me what they had spotted when going to town with mom. It never failed that on my bad days they could spot a number of unregistered snowmobiles or maybe even a party walking along a trout stream with a spear.

For some reason there was never a time when driving down the highway next to a trout stream I would see someone with a spear right next to the road.

It seems like a long time ago, but when my kids were growing up they always helped me out at the Hunter Safety Classes. In fact they always helped out at any classes that were held in my area and they loved helping dad.

The only bad thing about being the kids of a game warden is the fact that dad saw so many accidents where kids were either seriously hurt or even killed that he was maybe super cautious with his own children.

I guess it is human nature to be this way, but they really never understood having to wear life jackets in the bathtub.

I guess when dad has seen children trapped in campers when a fire started or accidents where a young lad shoots his cousin when out hunting in a boat you just get a different perspective on life.

I am almost willing to bet that my kids were the only ones in town that had to go through fire drills at home. We had it down to a science.

The girl's room was right at the top of the stairs going upstairs. Their older brothers were taught that in case of a fire it usually travels up a stairwell as the fire spreads. Each room had a smoke alarm. So if anything ever happened they were to get their sisters out of bed into their room. This was the first step in the fire drill.

After this, believe it or not, there was always an aluminum baseball bat in the corner of their bedroom. The boys were to take this baseball bat and break out the large front window over the front porch and get their sisters along with the two of them out on the roof of the porch. They were told by then dad would be there to help them down. For years after the boys were gone the bat still stood in the corner waiting just in case it was ever needed.

How many of the rest of you ever had fire drills in the house with dad making plans for the worst case scenario he could think of in life?

And here all these years you thought you had it bad with all the rules you had to put up with around the house with dad. Thank goodness we never had to really use the fire drill training in a real case of a fire, but life sure would have been a lot duller without dad around making sure everybody was ready just in case.

96

Our first buck taken on "Forty"

My retirement home during the fall of the year

Chapter 17

Conservation Officer's Stories
Upper Michigan Tales from a Game Warden's Perspective
I Won't Tell

While working all those nights as a game warden you were bound to run into some rather strange things. Here are some rather bazaar things that happened.

Not Again!

It seems that I went through a few years when there was always something trying to occupy the same spot that I was trying to occupy with my patrol unit. Needless to say there are those that are not impressed when this happens so you usually try to get around things another way.

On this evening we had been working shiners and had been running most of the time with our headlights out. We decided to take a 2-track trail through some state land that went through some heavy deer areas. We were still running without lights using the moonlight.

We had traveled a couple of miles back into this area when we came to an area where there were a lot of blueberries. Going through an area of blueberry bushes and poplar trees we saw the reflection of a vehicle pulled off the road in front of us.

As we came near this vehicle, still in the dark, we decided to go right by it and keep on going. The vehicle was running, we could see the exhaust, so I turned on my headlights to get by it on the 2-track.

As life would have it, just as we were clearing this "parked" vehicle the person in the car must have realized there was another vehicle on the road so he sat up pulled the car into reverse and backed into the side of the patrol car. Great!

After he pulled ahead I got out to see how much damage had been done to the back quarter panel of the unit. It was not too bad, but bad enough that I would have to do an accident report before I could get it fixed. Just what I needed.

The man got out of the car and walked back to where I was standing to see the damage. I knew who he was and after talking it over he ask me if I could get an estimate and he would just pay to get it fixed? I did not really care and was willing if only I did not have to do another accident report.

They had already come up with a retread driving school you had to attend if you had too many accident reports in a given period. This was one school I could live without.

So he told me he would be by about noon the next day to write me a check for the repair of the car. This would give me time to go by the body shop in the morning.

Noon came he didn't. Suppertime came and he didn't. About 8:00pm came and he didn't so I decided I had better go to plan B. Or else it looked like I would get stuck paying the bill seeing we had not made out an accident report.

I checked a few of his hangouts and there was no sign of him. Finally I went by his house, but he was not home. I told his wife that he was suppose to contact me at noon over an accident where he had backed into my patrol car.

She asked, "Where did it happen and which of our cars was he driving?" Right away I knew I was in trouble, so I just said, "When I was driving behind him when he was parked." She then said to me, "Up at the corner at the coffee shop I suppose, he's always up there drinking coffee." Now this was not a question requiring an answer so I did not volunteer one. She told me she would have him call me.

Oh' I did happen to mention that we had not made out an accident report because he was going to take care of the bill for the damages, but I had wrote down the license plate number off the car he was driving so we would know which one it was.

I took my time driving home because it was early evening and I was going through the game area.

Surprise when I got home he was sitting in my driveway with his checkbook. I showed him the estimate papers and he wrote out a check for the body shop that was going to fix it.

Oh' by the way, the license number off the car he had that night was not one of his maybe this was why he beat me home.

I Won't Tell

If you ever worked as a law enforcement officer one of the worst times you could have was when you had to go to court. For some reason it always seemed that the reason you ended up going to court never had anything to do with what took place.

As they used to say in one of the areas where I worked near one of the larger cities in Michigan, "Shoot your wife get probation, shoot a pheasant go to jail!" Sometimes you spent half the time just waiting for the legal maneuvering to get over.

I remember one case where we arrested a party that was standing by his car trunk with a loaded rifle in the middle of the night sighting in on a deer his buddy had froze in a spotlight beam. Inside the car we found some loaded handguns that had been stolen from a Detroit police officer's home.

The party hired a lawyer from Saginaw and we had our day in court. After umpteen meetings the party finally pled out to "unknowingly possessing a uncased firearm in an automobile". And the judge allowed him to plead to this!

Now there is no place in the whole wide universe where there is such a law as they came up with in this case on the books. It was one of those cases where the deal that was made had nothing to do with what happened. To top it off the party in this case had been caught shining for deer just down the road the year before. Oh' well there is nothing an officer can do in a case like this but say, "At least I did my job like it was suppose to be done.

But at times there are cases where the shoe is on the other foot. In one case I can remember where the defense attorney was trying to find something out from me when I was on the witness stand.

Now please remember that there are a lot of attorneys out there trying to defend people arrested for a fish or game violation when they have never hunted or fished in their life. This was true in this case.

We were in court trying a case of someone who was in possession of some illegal venison. We had a pretty good case and the crime lab had tied everything together for us. But there is almost always something that a good defense attorney can make a mountain out of if he can figure out how to do it. On this day this was the case. I had been on the stand for quite a while as the prosecutor laid out the whole case for the Jury. Now it was their turn.

The defense attorney ask me a number of questions about what had taken place and then got into what he hoped would be his defense for his client. So here we were getting into a new area.

He finally got to a point where he wanted to get some information out of me just as to how things had been handled. He hoped to show we did something wrong. I knew where he was trying to go, but he had no idea how to word the question to make me answer it with the answer he wanted to hear. He was in a mess.

I think the judge and those on the jury that hunted all saw where he was trying to go but they too knew he did not know how to get there when talking about hunting. But there was no way I was going to open the door for him when he could not ask the right question to receive the answer he wanted, so he never got it and we won the case. I guess it was the law of averages playing out.

You talk about being flustered, this attorney was, but the way the system works maybe he should have tried hunting and joined the NRA.

Right? Left?

Of course there are those times in life when you do not have the answer either. I have been caught in the middle of this problem too.

During this trial the prosecutor ask me which way the wind was from? Now this should be an easy question right? Not in my case.

I should have been able to answer this question right away just from what I had learned in college, but for some reason it was like one of those questions on a final exam where you just draw a blank. And remember the attorney that was asking this question was on my side.

So I answered the next best way I could think of and said, "From the right." Now this was true but not the answer he wanted. So he ask it a dozen different ways, but I could just not remember what direction the winds were from. After he ask me a dozen different ways and I came up with eleven dumb answers, the defense attorney jumped up and yelled, "I'll stipulate that the winds were out of the southwest on that day!" What could I say?

After the prosecutor got done the judge looked at me and said, "I would suggest you buy a compass".

Then there was the time we had the whole case laid out before a jury when the court took a break.

I had testified that the party was coming from the south going north when I pulled out and stopped them. At the break the court's magistrate came up to me and said, "John, I hate to differ with you but where you were that road runs east and west, US-2 there runs north and south for just more than a mile."

I looked at him and said, "I won't tell if you don't."

He looked at me and told me it was not his job to bring it up if the defense attorney did not catch it and he did not.

So you see sometimes there are things that happen in this world that you have no control over and other things you wish you did.

My Wifee

Me, after walking up a hill leaning
against a tree by our lake.

Chapter 18
Conservation Officer's Stories   **Upper Michigan Tales from a Game Warden's Perspective**
Gimmicks

I guess when you work for so many years as a Game Warden nothing should surprise you. But still you will run into things that have to make you wonder. Do they work? You can never really tell, but in a lot of cases if the person using this method of guarantee success thinks it works that is half the battle. Here are a few crazy things I have ran into or heard about.

Jugs

I guess one of the things that always amazed me was the number of jugs you would run into out on a lake marking someone's special fishing spot. Of course if you wanted to help them balance out the fish population on the lake you could always move their jug to another location on the lake.

Here is a story about a fisherman that had a different use for jugs that he claimed worked. It falls under I don't know, but just maybe, it might work, or I never tried that.

I was talking to a guy the other day that told me about a guy that always seemed to catch fish whenever he went out on the lake. It seemed that others could go out, fish the same areas, and have a so, so day. Nobody could figure out what his secret was. Of course there was no way he was going to tell.

But after some good field investigation it seems someone found out what his secret was. They noticed that whenever he went out he always had a couple of real clear containers. They also noticed that he always seemed to have more minnows than one person would ever need to take out fishing for just the couple hours he would go out in the evenings. So someone got in a position to watch him get ready to fish one day.

Before our always-successful fisherman even got any of his fishing gear together it seemed he took these two large, clear containers and filled them with water. Then he would split a large number of nice fishing minnows between these two containers and lower them into the water on both sides of the spot he was fishing.

Here he would sit for a minute or so as he got his pole and items ready and then he would start fishing right in the area where these two schools of minnows were swimming down there in the lake to attract fish!

Did it work? Was this the reason for all his fishing success? Will we ever really know? Or do we just have to say that no matter what this guy definitely had something going for him.

Of course you may not want to let certain people in the "Big House" know this trick or else they may have to do a study on baiting fish.

Flashbacks

I have said before that a Troll is really a sub-specie of a Yooper, but there are times when I have to wonder. In fact it is down right scary when you sit and read the headlines of some of the outdoor papers in this day and age. Maybe this material will help explain what I am getting at here.

Most of the outdoor papers and magazines you get now remind me of the newspapers by the checkout counters in the grocery stores. The ones that say something like, "Mrs. Clinton kissed by an alien from Mars!"

Let me give you a few examples of what we may have to look forward to if only a few of these articles end up happening.

1. Study shows perch in Great Lakes starving!
2. Treaty issues may give Indians greater hunting and inland lakes fishing rights!
3. Chronic Wasting Disease may wipe out deer herd!
4. Bovine TB found in deceased person!
5. Large oil spill on River Rouge!
6. Sports Afield magazine to stop publishing!
7. Turkey hunter recovers from bobcat attack!
8. Are Chicago area commercial fishermen taking all the Smelt?

This was all in one week in different papers doing articles on the outdoors. If I saw all these and a few more it makes a person wonder how many of these type articles are out there for the public to read?

It really scares this old fossil on what we may see come down the pike that will affect all of us that like our hunting and fishing? When you stop and think that 90% of those making the rules that affect all of us really never hunted or fished in their life, it sure scares a person. If this be the case, and it is in more cases than you know, then all the decisions are being make by those "Exspurts" behind a desk from a book.

I sat in on some of the Wisconsin DNR meetings down in Madison on the chronic wasting disease, and I can tell you for a fact that both there and here in Michigan a lot of these "Exspurts" never in their life sat out in the woods, in a blind, and just watched deer for hours to see what they would do! I don't mean just over a bait pile that some are blaming for all the problems, but deer moving around doing what comes naturally to wildlife.

A Wisconsin farmer that happened to be sitting next to me at this meeting looked at me after some of the remarks that were made and said, "You have to be kidding me, have they ever bothered to watch animals in a barnyard?" I swear some of them never have.

Get ready folks because we all may be sitting around camp talking about those "Good Old days" right after the turn of the century if some people get their way.

If I remember correctly Robin Hood was really being chased by the game warden because the King (the government) had put too many rules on deer hunting in Sherwood Forest. At least I think this was the way the story went back in the Stone Age when this old fossil was growing up over in Ontonagon.

I Thought Yoopers Were Smarter

You know I could see a Troll getting into a mess like this, but I really never figured a Yooper would ever find himself in this purdickerment. You read all the time in the real estate adds in the papers something that goes like this, "Nice hunting property, lots of low-lands with a nice building site".

Now this usually means that you are buying swampland with a pimple out in the middle of it somewhere that you can use for a building site. That is if you build during the dry season. But of course if you decide to build during the wet season you had better build a wood structure because wood floats and it is easier to find it.

Don't you think a person, especially a Yooper, would be a little suspicious of someone that told him about a "Good Deal" on some lakefront property when the lakefront property was on all four sides of the building site?

But if you should invest in some property like this with water on all four sides, I have heard that if you get some pieces of the largest plastic pipe you can find, the type they use for running trillions of wires through in a **big** building, cap off both ends, and fasten it securely to your 4-wheeler, you can float it into camp when you have a spring like we have at times in the U.P.

Then again a person could build a heliport on the pimple of high ground in this lakefront-hunting forty if it is big enough.

Now a Troll I could see, but I just never thought a Yooper would get into a mess like this. I just may have to redo my file on human nature.

PS:
By the way, someone asked Teivo last week, after reading the Fish Report. about the party that had to float into camp on his 4-wheeler, "When does a floating 4-wheeler become a motorized boat where you need a boat registration and a life jacket?" I really think life is getting way to involved for this Yooper!

So remember if you should see a sign "Good Hunting 40" you had better watch out because this could mean it is not good for anything else but hunting. And that hunting could be ducks!

Chapter 19

Conservation Officer's Stories
Upper Michigan Tales from a Game Warden's Perspective

My Opinion On Gun Control

The following three sections are articles I wrote on gun control. If you have spent your whole life living out in the backwoods both growing up there and later working as a Game Warden it should come as no surprise to people about how you feel about gun control.

So if the snow was flying, the north winds were blowing, and people were getting cabin fever, all I had to do was write an article on gun control to warm them up and make them forget about the cold, winter weather.

In these three *Fish Reports* you will read how I feel about gun control, my reply to all the letters to the editor, and the last one tells how we can solve the whole problem.

The Fish Report I Did On Gun Control

I keep hearing over and over that only those that really are against gun control are the hunters and people that enjoy shooting firearms as a sport in this country; personally I do not believe this is true. In the past two weeks I have been E-mailed items on gun control from as far away as Alaska and Florida. This on top of what I receive from this area. A lot of people feel what is taking place is just plain wrong; it has nothing to do with hunting, but our constitutional rights as citizens of the United States of America.

I want to ask you something, having attended a number of gun shows to try to sell some of my books, I get to visit with a lot of people. One thing that is very interesting has come up in the last couple of weeks. It seems that Smith & Wesson Firearm Company cut a deal with those in favor of gun control, I ask you why? You see for years this company used to be one of the top sellers of firearms to law enforcement. But they have lost this market on account of the type products they have been manufacturing in the last number of years. How could they get this market back? Cut a deal with

Now the question is, are those working out there protecting you going to now be issued an inferior firearm to protect you with? This could happen with the deal that was cut. Check around and see just how many officers if given a choice would want to be issued a firearm manufactured by this company.

Here are some interesting facts for those that think gun control will work in stopping crime. The key is who is going to decide what is classified as a crime?

Just over a year ago Australia forced the surrender of 604,381 personal firearms. This cost the government $500 million dollars.

The results you won't hear about in other places are these:
(1) Australia-wide, homicides up 3.2 percent
(2) Australia-wide, assaults are up 8.6 percent
(3) Australia-wide, armed robberies are up 44 percent, yes armed robberies almost doubled
(4) In the state of Victoria, homicides with firearms are up 300 percent. Yes, this report said up 300 percent using a firearm! Figures also showed that over the previous 25 years a steady decrease in armed robbery using a firearm, but this changed drastically in the past 12 months since gun control became the law. There was also a dramatic increase in break-ins and assaults of the elderly.

Does gun control work, if so we will be the first nation where it will. Here are some more facts sent to me.
(1) The Soviet Union established gun control in 1929, this caused 20 million people who didn't agree with those in power to be rounded up and disappear. I wonder what this means.
(2) Turkey established gun control in 1911. Within two years 1.5 million of those that didn't agree with those in power were rounded up and disappeared.
(3) Germany established gun control in 1938 and within years 13 million Jews and others that did not agree with those in power were rounded up and exterminated.
(4) China established gun control in 1935. Within years 20 million political dissidents (Those that didn't agree with those in power) were rounded up and disappeared.
(5) Guatemala established gun control in 1964. Within years

100,000 Mayan Indians were rounded up and exterminated.
(6) Uganda established gun control in 1970. Within a few years 300,000 Christians were rounded up and exterminated.
(7) Cambodia established gun control in 1956. Within two years one million people that didn't agree with those in power disappeared. Believe it or not these were mainly the "educated people" that were rounded up and killed.

This makes right around 56 million people that were rounded up and exterminated in the past century alone. Or should I say 56 million that we know about.

You see it is not only because I enjoy hunting that I am against "gun control". There is also the basic fact that what some people want to do is just wrong and will not work. I have taught Hunter's Safety for over thirty years and it makes me sick to see those that want to use "safety" as an excuse for passing gun control in our country. Do you really believe that a drug dealer would have a trigger lock on his illegal pistol? We had better wake up in this country or some other nation may be writing a list of facts about what happened to the United States after they passed "Gun Control" laws.

My Reply To The Letters To The Editor

I knew it! I knew it! Even before the article in the *Fish Report* on why there are some of us that feel the direction our nation is going on gun control will not work was printed, I knew I should have signed it "Grandpa Grizz"! I have never responded in almost twenty years of writing the *Fish Report* to a letter, but I guess it is time.

Right off the writer states he seldom reads the *Fish Report*, but then goes on and remarks about what was said in a number of them. I can understand this. When you really don't want someone out there to realize what you are doing you try to hide it from him or her. We used to call it the plain brown paper bag syndrome. It works like this; you take the section of the Tribune with the *Fish Report*, place it in a plain brown paper bag, and sneak it out into the garage to read it. After you are done you bury the paper, bag and all, out in the dog pen because you don't want anyone to know you are getting a little culture in your life.

Then this letter goes on to say I must have got my information off the Internet! Wow! Have I moved up in the world? Once again there is a problem with reading the *Fish Report* in the dark, I stated how I received the information. I am not hooked up to the Internet and have never been on the Internet. But I did watch someone using it in the Library one time. But then of course if I didn't get it from the unbelievable Internet, I must have got it from that cruel, mean, group of people called the NRA! Wrong again! But they are a good group to blame for anything you may not agree with. It's getting kind of old to blame things on Watergate anymore, so lets blame the NRA for everything.

Sub point: A lesson in life, never name something you are involved with, with a name that can be reduced to three letters. It is just too easy to make a swear word out of it. Like NRA! DNR!, if you don't agree with them. Also has the writer ever met the Executive Vice President Wayne LaPierre of the NRA to talk to him one on one? I guess I will have to admit it, one of the problems with writing the books I have is that I get to meet a whole lot of people that otherwise would never have crossed my path, Wayne Lapierre was one of these. To top it off I even got to shake hands with him. Now, where does this leave me if I say that he seemed like a regular person when you talk to him one on one.

Then he claims that those of us that worry about what is taking place are "alarmist". I wonder if there were any "alarmist" in Cambodia, Germany, and these other countries before they rewrote history with what happened? To say, "It could never happen here" is interesting, because I wonder if the people in these countries thought the same thing? Remember in some cases it was the well-educated people who were eliminated. I was at a dinner meeting as a speaker before a Historical Society one evening and part of their discussion was the fact that the local school district had dropped all history classes in favor of more art classes. Interesting, if you don't know about history the truth will soon be lost.

The one thing about this letter that really made my day was where he said that the Detroit Free Press had it right. I ask you one thing, when was the last time that the Detroit Free Press felt the same way about something as most of us that live in the U.P. do? If you think those in Washington are doing the right thing naturally you are going to agree with the Free Press.

In closing I must say that I find it rather interesting that those on a certain side of an issue are always right in the eyes of some people, but if you disagree with them in any way you are targeted as an "Alarmist". Is it not rather ludicrous to think that if trigger locks were mandatory that drug dealers, rapist, and other criminals would have them on their illegal firearms?

But when a statement like this is made by those in favor of gun controls some people do not even question it, I have to wonder. Besides the final tally averaged fourteen calls on the plus side from those that liked the information in the *Fish Report* to each negative comment in any form that was received about it.

Well, one good thing is that the writer of the letter should not read this *Fish Report* because in his own words, "I seldom read the *Fish Report* in the Tribune". So I am sure I am safe, but we will see. But, if he feels this way about gun control and all the lies told to support it, can you believe him when he says he never reads the *Fish Report*?

How To Solve The Whole Problem

Needless to say a lot of us that like our hunting and fishing are rather upset with the fact that people who own firearms are being cast in a bad light with all that has been going on in our country. But, I am one of those that believe the system that we now have with the young people is the main part of the problem.

Back in the Stone Age when I was attending high school Mr. Weber sure saw that the teenage boys towed the line. I could not even picture what he would have done if some of us did some of the things we see happening in high schools today.

I guess one of the key things that made this system work was the fact if you got into hot water at school you hoped and prayed that Dad never heard about it, or you went from not only hot water but to serious problems at home. I don't think Mr. Weber ever worried about the fact that most dads would not back him up in his discipline of the youth he was in charge of at school.

I guess thinking back, I am sure glad for the system I was a part of in growing up.

Another key item of growing up back then was the fact that one day each week school was let out early and we would go to the church we attended on Sunday for classes put on by the church.

I am sure thankful back then for Father Bennett and Father Oliver and the love they had for the teenage boys that crossed their path. I can still remember so many things Father Bennett warned us about and the things he taught us during those classes. Father Oliver and some other men took us to the biggest city in the U.P. where he was from when they were filming the movie Antomny of Murder.

I remember that the car we rode in was a 58 Chevy, with a 348 souped up motor in it. I had never ridden in anything that ran like this did. But the key was, they also made and taught us to behave.

I can also remember like it was yesterday being marched over to the large back porch where the Nuns lived to get to do a little after hours project we had managed to qualify for. They would call our parents and tell them we would be a little late getting home and once again our parents backed up the system. In fact I had to wonder at times if I spent more time on this back porch or in school.

But you know it never crossed my mind that just maybe, these people were violating my constitutional rights against false imprisonenment. Or the fact that Mr. Weber did not realize that it is unconstitutional to correct us without proper representation and a fair trial with a jury of our piers.

In fact if the truth was known, I am not sure a teenager that grew up back when I did had any constitutional rights. There were rules and you were expected to obey them, if not there was a price to pay. The funny thing is that we never doubted that, when we saw Mr. Weber personally or were marched over to that famous back porch, but we knew we had done something to earn this opportunity.

There is no doubt in my mind some fifty years down the road that what these people did for us made us better people and citizens down the road.

The funny thing is, I thought we were keeping all this from Mom and Dad, but come to find out they knew everything we did and the results we received for doing it. There were a lot of laughs years later when Dad reminded me of those times.

You see I don't believe it's the fact one owns or does not own a firearm. I think it is the system one grows up in. You see I grew up right after the big war and remember those coming home from the Korean War. Guns were a way of life where and when I grew up, but some of the things that are going on today never crossed our minds.

You see there was a clear right and wrong back then and you soon learned where the line was. The programs you listened too on the radio made sure the good guy won in the end. Most movies made sense to a teenage boy or else they were just stupid and wrote off as, "It's only a movie."

The church taught you what movies were good and what was not. You never questioned Mom, Dad, or the Church in these matters. You knew what they were doing was for your benefit and to make you a better person.

You know that years later the boys that crossed Mr. Weber's path always talked about him with a kind of respect and were thankful for him.

You can outlaw guns, you can do all you want, but if the system is broken down these things will not fix it. In order to fix a broken system we have to return to the things that made it work in the first place.

You may not agree with me, but I was working in the system as things changed and the old values were tossed aside for what we have now. I saw the cracks come and the system break and there is no doubt in my mind how to help fix it. But the question is, is it going to happen?

Backwoods Glossary

Conservation Officer's Stories
Upper Michigan Tales from a Game Warden's
Perspective

Up here in the Great North Woods, there is a tendency to use terms or phrases to make a point. To some of you, they may be used in a way you never realized they could be. Other words or terms, you may just have not had the opportunity to ever use. This Backwoods Glossary is to help you out in understanding why we talk like we do.

U.P. (Upper Michigan): If, for some strange reason, you have never traveled in Michigan, these two letters would seem strange to you. First, understand that Michigan has two peninsulas the upper and lower. The Lower Peninsula is made up of two parts, Lower Michigan and Northern Michigan. But, the really important part of Michigan lies across the Mackinaw Bridge. This part of Michigan is called the U.P., for the Upper Peninsula of Michigan. The people up here in the U.P. live in their own little world and like it that way. The only problem is that most of the laws are passed down in Lower Michigan to correct their problems, and then they affect us, who may not even be part of that problem. Some of the Big City folks that pass these laws never have learned to understand and love the U.P. like we that live here do. The natives of the U.P. have trouble understanding the "why-for" about some of these laws; therefore they feel they really must not apply to them.

Two of the biggest industries in the U.P. are paper mills and the men that work in the woods supplying trees to these mills so they can produce their product. There are probably more colleges in the U.P., per capita, than anywhere else in the country. But even with this, there are still a lot of natives up here that feel you could sure ruin a good person if you sent them to one of these colleges. News of a serious crime will travel from one side of the U.P. to the other like a wild fire. Because most people up here are not used to it. To them, serious crimes are when someone takes a deer or some fish illegally and is dumb enough to get caught. They don't even take these crimes to seriously unless the poacher should step over the line and get to greedy.

Sports teams that play teams from other towns in the U.P. always seem to have relatives, or friends, on the other team. Everyone knows someone, or someone that married someone, that knew someone from over there. To win a state championship, you have to beat those teams from "down state". To do this is a dream come true for any red-blooded U.P. boy or girl.

When I was growing up, we had only had part-time radios. So we had to be Green Bay (Wisconsin) Packer and Milwaukee Brave fans. As a boy living in the Western U.P., we could not pick up any radio stations that carried broadcast of the teams from Lower Michigan. For this reason, we grew up feeling that we were a state unto ourselves. We could not be part of Lower Michigan, because it was just to far away, and the only way to get there was by boat. We knew we were not part of Wisconsin, so we were just the Good Old U.P.

Up here in the U.P., where life is tough, but things are good, and it is just a great place to live.

Some Backwoods (U.P.) Terms:

2-TRACK:(roads) The U.P. has hundreds of miles of this type of roads. All these roads consist of are two tire ruts worn into the ground from all the vehicle travel throughout the years. Usually you have a high, grass-covered center and mud holes in the low spots. This is one of the reasons that so many people in the U.P. feel you cannot live without a 4x4 pickup. These roads are never worked on or improved and you get what you see.

Blacktop Roads: These are the 2-tracks, which are worse than unimproved roads. They are covered by mud or clay and it is a real trick to stay between the trees on some of these. There are also a lot of these type roads for which the U.P. is famous. Many a fishermen or hunter has spent hours and hours trying to get out of one of these blacktop roads, usually after you misjudged what you were getting into. Two of the first things I learned after becoming a Game Warden stationed in the U.P. were: It's hard to get 2-ton stuck at fifty miles an hour, so wind it up and keep moving. The other one follows point one, you are never really stuck till you stop. In other words, if one of these blacktop areas sneaks up on you, floor it and don't stop 'til you reach high ground or hit something unmovable.

Poachers: These are not people that cook eggs in hot water, but may get themselves in hot water now and then. They are outlaws that rob the honest hunters and fishermen of their chance to get game and fish legally. In years past, it was a way of life in the U.P. that was passed down from generation to generation. When it was an accepted thing to do, the Game Warden not only had a hard time catching the poachers, but he usually had an even harder time trying to get a conviction in the local courts.

Shining: (Shinning, Shining, Shiners), Shiners are the poachers that use a spotlight to look for deer at night, in order to shoot them. Until the fines got to high, it was the way that a lot of the outlaws did their hunting here in the U.P. They would take a pair of spot-lights, hook them up in their vehicle, and then drive around while casting the rays of the spotlights out into fields or an old orchard, until they spotted a deer. The deer, blinded by the bright light, would stand there staring at the light while the poacher got out his gun and shot it. There is really no sport in it, because it is so dead-ly. You will notice I spelled shinning, with two "n's" at times. Well, I did this on my tickets for dozens of cases throughout the years; until a State Trooper told me it was spelled wrong. He said it should only have one "n", so on the next couple tickets I changed how I spelled shining. You see for years, when I caught someone hunt-ing deer at night with a spotlight, the only thing I would write for a charge on the ticket was the one word "shinning". With the one word spelled, Shinning, they knew what they did, I knew what they had done, and most important the average U.P. Judge knew what they were standing before him for doing. Well, the first time I caught a crew out spotlighting for deer and put shining (with one n) on their ticket they pled "Not Guilty". The spelling must have con-fused them and so was I.

Spearers: These are people that have a way of taking fish with the use of a spear. The spear can have from three to five prongs, with pointed tips; these prongs have barbs on the end to hold the fish on the spear after they spear it. Now in some areas, it is legal to spear certain types of non-game fish. The problem the Game Warden has is with those that spear trout, salmon, walleye, etc. or "game fish". When these fish come into real shallow water to spawn, a Game Warden will spend hour after hour watching the fish spawning in these areas.

Extractors: This is a term for those illegal fishermen that may come along a creek with a spear trying to extract the spawning fish from the creek. They may use other devices besides a spear. For instance, a weighted hook, hand nets, their hands, etc.

Gill Netters: These are people, both legal and illegal, that use a gill net to take fish. In some areas, there is a commercial fishery allowed with the use of gill nets, but in Michigan it is never legal for "sport" fishermen to use a gill net to take fish. A gill net is made up of nylon string in little squares (it looks something like a small woven wire fence) built so the fish will swim into the net putting their head through the square openings. Then, they get caught when their larger body will not fit through the squares and their gills keep them from backing out of the nets. I have observed illegal gill net fishermen take hundreds of pounds of steelhead in a couple of hours, if they set their gill nets in the right spot.

Fish house or fish shed: In areas of the U.P., along the great lakes where there is a legal commercial fishery, most of those businesses involved have a building where they clean, box in ice, and store their catch. They may also repair their nets in this building. On account of the smell around a full time commercial fishing operation, most of these sheds are located away from any residence. They also may be on the riverbank where the commercial fisherman ties up his fish tug. For this reason they are often used for illegal activity, sometimes by others than those that own them.

Deer camp: A deer camp can be any type of building used for offering protection from the elements. It is also used as a "get-a-way from home during the hunting season. Some are as nice as any house, better than some, while others may be made out of plastic, heavy paper, scrap lumber, or anything to keep the weather out. The following rules are some of the usual type that are proper for deer camp life.

(1) You cannot shave or take a bath, no matter how many days you may be staying at camp. You are allowed to wash your face and hands. But this is your own choice; you do not have to if you do not want to. This is one reason young boys love to go to deer camp with Dad.

(2) There is no proper way to dress while at deer camp, if it feels good wear it! You can even wear the same clothes all week long. This includes your socks, if you can catch them after the first three days at camp.

(3) The "menu" is always made up of all the "proper" things that you cannot afford to eat all the rest of the year at home. Both good and bad for you.

(4) It is never wrong to tell a "true" story on another camp member. Remembering it is of more value if you can dress it up a little to make him suffer all the time you are telling it. During the telling of his misfortune we must all remember that we will all pay for our mistakes, sooner or later, if and when our hunting "buddies" find out about them.

(5) It is a crime, punishable by banishment, to talk about school, or schoolwork, or any work for that matter while at deer camp.

(6) You can throw, hang or just leave your socks and clothes any-where they land when you remove them. You can hang your wet socks on anything that has something to hang them from to try and dry them out before the next days hunt. Always remembering it is "most" important to have dry socks by daybreak the next morning.

(7) What may be called work at home is not work at deer camp. Therefore getting things done at deer camp is not classified as work, but a team effort. For this reason, it is not wrong for a boy to do dishes, sweep a floor, pick up trash (that he missed getting in the trash can when he threw it that way, with one of his famous hook shots), or even do what Dad asks him to do, the first time Dad asks him to do it.

You would have to spend a week at a real U.P. deer camp to real-ly know the true feeling of being a U.P. deer hunter. With these easy-to-apply rules, you can see why deer camp life is so impor-tant to a boy during his informative teenage years. It is really important that a young man start out with a proper perspective on life.

Big House: This is the Michigan State Capital; from some areas of the U.P. it can be over 400 miles away. In Lansing, this is where "they" compile all the rules and ideas that are put out to confuse the average hunter or fisherman, while out in the field. It is the feeling of a lot of U.P. sportsmen, that most of those that work down there, in Lansing's Big House, never in their lives set foot in the real out-of-doors, or wet a fishing line in a back woods stream. What they know, they got from someone that wrote a book without ever having set their feet in a real woods, or having gone backwoods fishing either. It is just passed on from desk to desk, year after year, put into volumes of rules and law books that we out in the field have to learn to live with. This while trying to enjoy ourselves out in the real Northwood's, Michigan's U.P.

Wifee: (W-IF-EE; wify) this is one's wife. To pronounce it right, you say the "W" sound, then the "IF", then draw out the "EE".

Big Lake: This can be any of the Great Lakes that border Michigan. Instead of saying, " I went fishing out on Lake Michigan Saturday". A native from the U.P. would say, "I went fishing on the Big Lake Saturday afternoon".

Off-road vehicles: ATV'S, ORV'S, dirt bikes, etc. These may be any of the type vehicles that are made primarily to operate off an improved road. Some may be homemade, while dealers sell others. In the U.P. you will find a lot of these used by sportsmen to get around when hunting and fishing.

Game Wardens: Conservation Officer, C.O.'s, and Game Wardens are all one and the same, up here in the U.P. They have been around for better than 100 years serving the people of Michigan. The stories they can tell and those told on them are told over and over around the U.P. This is how my newspaper, story telling got started.

Holiday Stations: Holiday? Here, in Michigan's U.P., you always hear the expression, "I'm going to stop by Holiday on the way". Some of you folks may not understand what a Holiday is and how far advanced the U.P. is over other areas of our country. I'll try to explain. Holiday; here in the North Country is a gas station-store. The Holiday Stations have been around for years and years, and in the U.P. they are like a mini-mall. The U.P. and Holiday were way ahead of the rest of the world on this idea of doing all your shopping in one stop. Get your gas plus whatever else you may need here at the Holiday. Sometimes it just takes awhile for you all to catch up to us, Yoopers.

Years ago when Christmas time came around, you went down to the Holiday. Here you did all your Christmas shopping. It had a great toy selection, in fact, in most U.P. towns the best to be found. If company dropped in for a surprise visit and you needed food items, off you went to the Holiday to get what you needed. When hunting and fishing season rolled around, they put out a paper and sales ad to get you into the Holiday to fill your needs, everything from guns and ammo, to poles, hooks, and line. If you snagged your waders, off you went to the Holiday for new ones. If your feet got cold out deer hunting, off to the Holiday for warm footgear you went. If your motorized deer blind broke down on a weekend, off to the auto parts section of the Holiday to get what you needed. What am I saying? Before the rest of the world was smart enough to think about putting other than gas and oil supplies in their gas stations the Holiday was there. Now they have moved up one more step because most Holiday Stations have copies of my books for sale.

Remember when traveling through the U.P., if a town does not have a Holiday station, keep on trucking till you find one because that town you are in has not arrived yet!

Copper Country: In so many parts of my book, you will read about things that took place in the Copper Country. This area covers what is called the Keweenaw Peninsula over to the area of the copper mines to the west. Those of us that lived in the Copper Country felt you were going into the world of the great unknown if you left Ontonagon, Houghton, Baraga, or Keweenaw County. In fact, a person growing up when I did may have left the Copper Country for the first time when he went into the service. The Copper Country is really a melting pot of people from all over the world. When I was growing up, it was nothing for some of the old folks not being able to speak English; they talked in their native language. In fact, one of the things that really bugged a teenage boy from the Copper Country was when there were a couple of girls your buddy and you wanted to get to know, and they would talk back and forth in Finnish, and we did not have the foggiest idea what they were saying. The history of the Copper Country is both interesting and unreal if you study it. A person could move away and be gone for years, but when asked where they are from, they always answer the Copper Country.

In the Copper Country, everybody knows somebody that knows somebody else. When on a radio show talking about my first book, "*A Deer Gets Revenge*", a party called in and wanted to know if I was Harry Theiler's grandson. Then another party called in and wanted to know if I was Tim Walker's brother. (Tim is my brother that lives in a home in Hancock, MI, in the Copper Country). Copper Country people are special people that help make up a place called the U.P. where people know and care about each other. Come visit the U.P. and Copper Country someday, and you will see what I mean.

The other day: I keep telling my kids and the readers of my newspaper article that when I use the saying, "The other day", it could mean anytime between birth and death. It is up to the person you are talking too, to try and figure out what era you are talking about. Up here in the U.P., a party could start to tell you a hunting story by saying, " *The other day a buddy and I....*" and the story may have taken place back in the forties. (1940's) You have to remember that good stories never really get old; they just get better and added to in the telling of them. There was one officer I worked with could he tell stories! He would get going into a story and you would sit there and listen. Pretty soon bits and pieces would start to ring a bell. Then all of a sudden it would dawn on you that you were with him when "his story" took place, but you really never remembered it happening like he was telling it, or could it have? One of my boys called me from college a while back (another one of those times that means nothing in U.P. phrases) to ask me about the history of the 60's. This was for a paper he had to do for a history course. I told him, "Son, the 60's do not qualify as history yet. That is when your dad says, you know the other day, or awhile back, and that makes it today not history."

Exspurt: Sometimes in the U.P. we have our own way of spelling and understanding things. Here is one of those terms. I have a buddy that is a U.P. potato farmer. (You have to really wonder about anybody that tries to farm in the U.P.) But this buddy has a great definition for all those exspurts that rule down in the Big House. It is one of those terms you have to think about, but the more you think about it, the more you feel that this potato farmer may go down in history as a great U.P. philosopher. We will get talking about all those rules and laws the exspurts down in Lansing and Washington pass that are totally unreal, and my buddy will say, "Always remember that an ex-spurt is only a drip under pressure!" Now, I wonder.....

But then, you have all these TV shows on with an outdoor Exspurt on just about everything. Let's be real now. Do they ever get skunked out there fishing? Do you ever see them spending all day baiting hooks for the kids and getting the kids' lines untangled? Or get the boat unloaded and the motor won't start? Somehow, someway, I get the feeling these exspurts have never hunted or fished out there in the real world.

Let me give you an example of an Exspurt. One night I happened to be going through the cable channels and came across this Exspurt fisherman who had his own TV show. It happened that on this show he was fishing an area off Lake Superior that I was in charge of, so I decided to watch this show. Here is our Exspurt telling people how it should be done and where the nice steelhead fishing is in the U.P. As I watched, I couldn't believe it. So I got on the phone and called a Conservation Officer that worked for me and worked the area in the program. I told him, "John, you blew it and missed one. "He replied, "You must be watching the same program I'm watching." Then we both had a good laugh. Why? Because here was this Exspurt going along a trout stream running out of Lake Superior with an illegal device used to take trout in the spring of the year in that area! I told John, "Maybe we ought to send him a ticket in the mail. We have what he's doing on film, and he is even telling us he's doing it. "But you have to understand that this fishing Exspurt was a "troll"(a person that lives below the Big Mac Bridge.), and therefore, you get what you pay for. Now, remember what an Exspurt is, "A drip under pressure", and life will be a lot easier to understand.

Huskavarina edumacation; There has always been a feeling that there is more wisdom learned at the back end of a chain saw than you learn in college. The more some of us see and hear what is going on in our country, the more we have to wonder. It was always an amazement to those that worked out in the field for the government to see someone go off to the "Big House" on a promotion and forget everything they learned out in the field in the first six-months they were there! In fact, some of us always felt that about halfway down through the lower peninsula there was an invisible force field that made up a brain sucking machine, and by the time they passed through this going to the "Big House", they were useless to us living in the U.P.

We used to suggest that everyone after about a year or two down in Lansing's or Washington's "Big House" ought to have to spend six months back in the woods on the working end of a chain saw to get the feeling for how the real world lives again. That is why the U.P. is a special place, because from the woods, to the mines, to the papers mills, most of its people have a Husavarina Edumacation.

Sometimes I think it makes them special people as you can see by some of my stories.

Bugs: Back when I was a kid, a bug was not an insect. It was something you rode in going hunting. (Look at the picture in the books of us hunting in the 40's and 50's, and you will see our Bug.) You would take an old Model T or A and put oversize tires on it to raise it up off the ground. Then you would find some old tire chains. Most of the time they had no body left on them, and you were to hang on for dear life when you came to a big mud hole. A party always had this saying, "It's hard to get two-tons stuck at fifty miles an hour, but when you do you are really stuck." I always said, "You are never stuck till you stop, so the key is never to stop till you hit high ground again." All the hunters used these vehicles back before anyone ever heard of a 4x4 pickup. They were homemade, and you were really someone when you had one. In fact I cannot count the times we gave the Game Warden a ride back into the backcountry when he had something to check on because he was not lucky enough to own a "Bug". But, now if a person was to make one and try to use it, they would end up having to hire a secretary to file the nine thousand-four hundred-seventy-five million tickets you would receive for having this dangerous vehicle back in the woods. Man, those were the good old days; No ORV laws, no snowmobile laws, about half the hunting laws, and no Big Mac bridge to let all those idealists across into God's country.

Yoopers: Have you ever been asked, "What's a Yooper?" It seems that there are certain terms that the real world has not used yet. If you take the Upper Peninsula of Michigan abbreviated, namely "The U.P. and sound it out what do you get? It has to be the word Yooper. Therefore all the good people (natives only) that make their homes in the U.P. of Michigan have to be Yooper. Right?

Up here in Yooper Country we have our own jokes, our own Yooper singing groups, our own terms, and a great life style.

The one thing that you want to remember is that you are born a True Yooper. It cannot be bought, you cannot get it by living here for years and years, and you must be born a Yooper. We have a real problem with Trolls (Those that live below the Big Mac Bridge.) coming up to Yooper land then trying to act like or become one of us, it just cannot be done! You either have it or you don't. You can come see us, we are glad when you spend your money here, we like you for a friend, but remember when you leave Yooper Land you leave as you came, not as a Yooper.

Order Form

There are now seven great books in the *Tales From A Game Warden series.* They can be ordered in a set or single copies from: JAW'S Publications, 530 Alger Ave. Manistique, MI 49854. Phone number: 906-341-2082. E-mail address: jawspub@juno.com A single copy cost $10.00 plus $2.50 for shipping and handling or a complete set of all seven books for $50.00, plus $2.50 for shipping and handling.

Book #
1. A Deer Gets Revenge ISBN 0-9639798-0-9
2. A Bucket Of Bones ISBN 0-9639798-1-7
3. Land of Big Fish ISBN 0-9639798-2-5
4. Luck, Skill, Stupidity ISBN 0-9639798-0-9639798-3-3
5. Humans Are Nuts! ISBN 0-9639798-4-
6. But Honey It Wasn't My Fault! ISBN 0-9639798-6-8
7. Whatdaya Mean A Bad Attitude! ISBN 0-9639798-7-6

126